Feathers and Flavours

Global Chicken Recipes for Every Palate

Table of contents

34. Moroccan Chicken Bastilla
35. Thai Red Curry Chicken
36. Jamaican Curry Chicken
37. Lebanese Chicken Fatteh
38. Turkish Chicken Pilaf (Tavuk Pilavı)
39. Vietnamese Lemongrass Chicken
40. Argentinean Chicken Milanesa
41. Filipino Chicken Tinola
42. Ethiopian Doro Tibs
43. Russian Chicken Kotleti
44. Thai Chicken Larb
45. Cuban Chicken Fricassee
46. Pakistani Chicken Karahi
47. Malaysian Chicken Rendang
48. Italian Chicken Marsala
49. Greek Chicken Gyro
50. Japanese Chicken Yakitori
51. Indian Chicken Tikka Masala
52. Spanish Chicken Paella Valenciana
53. Korean Spicy Chicken Stew (Dakdoritang)
54. Brazilian Chicken Stroganoff
55. Mexican Chicken Tinga
56. Moroccan Chicken Couscous
57. Thai Pineapple Chicken Curry
58. Jamaican Brown Stew Chicken
59. Lebanese Garlic Chicken (Djaj Mhammar)
60. Turkish Chicken Iskender

Recipe 1: Italian Chicken Parmesan

Preparation Time: 15 minutes
Cooking Time: 25 minutes
Total Time: 40 minutes
Servings: 4

Ingredients:
- 4 boneless, skinless chicken breasts
- Salt and pepper to taste
- 1 cup all-purpose flour
- 2 large eggs, beaten
- 1 cup breadcrumbs
- 1 cup grated Parmesan cheese
- 2 cups marinara sauce
- 1 cup shredded mozzarella cheese
- Fresh basil leaves for garnish

Instructions:
1. Preheat the oven to 400°F (200°C). Grease a baking dish with cooking spray.
2. Season the chicken breasts with salt and pepper.
3. Set up three shallow bowls: one with flour, one with beaten eggs, and one with a mixture of breadcrumbs and grated Parmesan cheese.
4. Dredge each chicken breast in the flour, then dip into the beaten eggs, and finally coat with the breadcrumb-Parmesan mixture, pressing gently to adhere.
5. Place the coated chicken breasts in the prepared baking dish. Bake in the preheated oven for 20 minutes.

6. Remove the chicken from the oven and spoon marinara sauce over each breast. Sprinkle shredded mozzarella cheese on top.
7. Return the baking dish to the oven and bake for an additional 5 minutes, or until the cheese is melted and bubbly.
8. Garnish with fresh basil leaves before serving.

Serving Suggestion: Serve the Italian Chicken Parmesan hot with a side of spaghetti tossed in marinara sauce and a sprinkle of extra Parmesan cheese. Pair with a crisp green salad dressed with balsamic vinaigrette for a complete meal.

Recipe 2: Japanese Chicken Teriyaki

Preparation Time: 10 minutes
Cooking Time: 15 minutes
Total Time: 25 minutes
Servings: 4

Ingredients:
- 4 boneless, skinless chicken thighs or breasts
- Salt and pepper to taste
- 1/2 cup soy sauce
- 1/4 cup mirin (Japanese sweet rice wine)
- 2 tablespoons sake (Japanese rice wine) or dry sherry
- 2 tablespoons sugar
- 1 tablespoon vegetable oil
- 2 green onions, thinly sliced, for garnish
- Sesame seeds for garnish (optional)

Instructions:
1. Season the chicken thighs or breasts with salt and pepper.
2. In a small bowl, whisk together soy sauce, mirin, sake, and sugar until the sugar is dissolved to make the teriyaki sauce.
3. Heat vegetable oil in a large skillet over medium heat. Add the seasoned chicken to the skillet and cook until browned on both sides, about 5-6 minutes per side.
4. Pour the teriyaki sauce over the chicken in the skillet. Reduce heat to low and simmer for another 5-7 minutes, or until the sauce thickens and coats the chicken.

5. Remove the chicken from the skillet and let it rest
for a few minutes before slicing.
6. Serve the sliced chicken drizzled with extra teriyaki
sauce from the skillet. Garnish with sliced green
onions and sesame seeds, if desired.

Serving Suggestion: Serve the Japanese Chicken
Teriyaki over steamed white rice, alongside sautéed
vegetables such as broccoli, carrots, and snap peas.
Sprinkle with additional sesame seeds and serve with
pickled ginger on the side for a traditional Japanese
touch.

Recipe 3: Indian Butter Chicken (Murgh Makhani)

Preparation Time: 20 minutes
Cooking Time: 30 minutes
Total Time: 50 minutes
Servings: 4

Ingredients:
- 4 boneless, skinless chicken breasts, cut into bite-sized pieces
- Salt and pepper to taste
- 1/4 cup plain yogurt
- 2 tablespoons lemon juice
- 2 tablespoons garam masala
- 1 tablespoon ground cumin
- 1 tablespoon ground coriander
- 1 teaspoon turmeric
- 1/2 teaspoon cayenne pepper (adjust to taste)
- 4 tablespoons butter
- 1 onion, finely chopped
- 3 cloves garlic, minced
- 1 tablespoon grated fresh ginger
- 1 cup tomato puree
- 1 cup heavy cream
- Fresh cilantro leaves for garnish

Instructions:
1. In a bowl, combine yogurt, lemon juice, garam masala, ground cumin, ground coriander, turmeric, cayenne pepper, salt, and pepper. Add chicken pieces and toss to coat. Marinate for at least 1 hour in the refrigerator.

2. In a large skillet, melt 2 tablespoons of butter over medium heat. Add the marinated chicken pieces and cook until browned on all sides, about 5-6 minutes. Remove the chicken from the skillet and set aside.
3. In the same skillet, melt the remaining 2 tablespoons of butter. Add chopped onion, minced garlic, and grated ginger. Cook until the onions are soft and translucent, about 5 minutes.
4. Stir in tomato puree and cook for another 5 minutes, stirring occasionally.
5. Return the cooked chicken to the skillet and stir to combine with the tomato mixture. Pour in heavy cream and simmer for 10-15 minutes, or until the sauce has thickened slightly.
6. Garnish with fresh cilantro leaves before serving.

Serving Suggestion: Serve the Indian Butter Chicken hot over a bed of basmati rice, garnished with additional cilantro leaves. Accompany with warm naan bread or roti for dipping into the creamy sauce.

Recipe 4: Thai Chicken Pad Thai

Preparation Time: 20 minutes
Cooking Time: 10 minutes
Total Time: 30 minutes
Servings: 4

Ingredients:
- 8 ounces rice noodles
- 2 tablespoons vegetable oil
- 2 cloves garlic, minced
- 8 ounces boneless, skinless chicken breast, thinly sliced
- 2 eggs, lightly beaten
- 2 cups bean sprouts
- 1/4 cup chopped green onions
- 1/4 cup chopped roasted peanuts
- Lime wedges for serving

For Pad Thai Sauce:
- 3 tablespoons fish sauce
- 2 tablespoons tamarind paste
- 2 tablespoons brown sugar
- 1 tablespoon soy sauce
- 1 teaspoon chili paste (adjust to taste)

Instructions:
1. Cook rice noodles according to package instructions until al dente. Drain and set aside.
2. In a small bowl, whisk together fish sauce, tamarind paste, brown sugar, soy sauce, and chili paste to make the Pad Thai sauce. Set aside.

3. Heat vegetable oil in a large skillet or wok over medium-high heat. Add minced garlic and cook for 30 seconds until fragrant.
4. Add sliced chicken breast to the skillet and stir-fry until cooked through, about 4-5 minutes.
5. Push the chicken to one side of the skillet and pour beaten eggs into the other side. Scramble the eggs until cooked, then mix with the chicken.
6. Add cooked rice noodles and Pad Thai sauce to the skillet. Toss everything together until well combined and heated through.
7. Stir in bean sprouts and chopped green onions, cooking for an additional 1-2 minutes.
8. Remove from heat and sprinkle chopped roasted peanuts over the top.
9. Serve hot with lime wedges on the side for squeezing over the Pad Thai.

Serving Suggestion: Serve the Thai Chicken Pad Thai garnished with additional chopped peanuts and fresh cilantro. Pair with a refreshing cucumber salad or Thai spring rolls for a complete Thai-inspired meal.

Recipe 5: Mexican Chicken Enchiladas

Preparation Time: 20 minutes
Cooking Time: 25 minutes
Total Time: 45 minutes
Servings: 4

Ingredients:
- 2 cups shredded cooked chicken (rotisserie chicken works well)
- 1 cup shredded Monterey Jack cheese, divided
- 1 cup shredded cheddar cheese, divided
- 1 can (10 ounces) enchilada sauce
- 1/2 cup chopped onion
- 1/4 cup chopped fresh cilantro
- 1 teaspoon ground cumin
- 1/2 teaspoon garlic powder
- 1/2 teaspoon chili powder
- 8 small corn tortillas
- Sliced jalapeños for garnish (optional)
- Sour cream and chopped fresh cilantro for serving

Instructions:
1. Preheat the oven to 350°F (175°C). Grease a 9x13-inch baking dish with cooking spray.
2. In a large bowl, combine shredded chicken, 1/2 cup Monterey Jack cheese, 1/2 cup cheddar cheese, chopped onion, chopped cilantro, ground cumin, garlic powder, and chili powder. Mix well.
3. Warm the corn tortillas in the microwave for 20-30 seconds to make them pliable.

4. Spoon a generous amount of the chicken mixture onto each tortilla and roll up tightly. Place the filled tortillas seam-side down in the prepared baking dish.
5. Pour enchilada sauce over the top of the rolled tortillas, spreading it evenly to cover.
6. Sprinkle the remaining shredded Monterey Jack and cheddar cheeses over the enchiladas.
7. Bake in the preheated oven for 20-25 minutes, or until the cheese is melted and bubbly.
8. Garnish with sliced jalapeños, if desired, and chopped fresh cilantro.
9. Serve hot with sour cream on the side.

Serving Suggestion: Serve the Mexican Chicken Enchiladas with Mexican rice and refried beans. Top with additional enchilada sauce, sour cream, and chopped fresh cilantro for extra flavour. Enjoy with a side of crunchy tortilla chips and salsa for a festive Mexican fiesta.

Recipe 6: French Coq au Vin

Preparation Time: 20 minutes
Cooking Time: 2 hours
Total Time: 2 hours 20 minutes
Servings: 6

Ingredients:
- 6 chicken thighs, bone-in and skin-on
- Salt and pepper to taste
- 6 slices of bacon, chopped
- 1 onion, chopped
- 2 carrots, chopped
- 2 cloves garlic, minced
- 1 cup mushrooms, sliced
- 2 cups red wine (such as Pinot Noir or Burgundy)
- 1 cup chicken broth
- 2 tablespoons tomato paste
- 1 teaspoon dried thyme
- 2 bay leaves
- Fresh parsley for garnish

Instructions:
1. Season the chicken thighs with salt and pepper.
2. In a large Dutch oven or heavy-bottomed pot, cook the chopped bacon over medium heat until crispy. Remove the bacon and set aside, leaving the rendered fat in the pot.
3. Add the chicken thighs to the pot and brown on both sides, about 5 minutes per side. Remove the chicken and set aside.
4. Add chopped onion, carrots, and minced garlic to the pot. Cook until the vegetables are softened, about 5 minutes.

5. Stir in sliced mushrooms and cook for another 3-4 minutes.
6. Return the cooked bacon to the pot. Add red wine, chicken broth, tomato paste, dried thyme, and bay leaves. Bring to a simmer.
7. Return the browned chicken thighs to the pot, making sure they are submerged in the liquid. Cover and simmer over low heat for 1.5 to 2 hours, until the chicken is tender and cooked through.
8. Remove the bay leaves and discard. Adjust seasoning with salt and pepper if needed.
9. Serve hot, garnished with fresh parsley.

Serving Suggestion: Coq au Vin is traditionally served with crusty French bread or over mashed potatoes to soak up the rich sauce. Pair with a side of green beans or steamed vegetables for a complete French-inspired meal.

Recipe 7: Moroccan Chicken Tagine

Preparation Time: 20 minutes
Cooking Time: 1 hour
Total Time: 1 hour 20 minutes
Servings: 4

Ingredients:
- 4 chicken thighs, bone-in and skin-on
- Salt and pepper to taste
- 2 tablespoons olive oil
- 1 onion, thinly sliced
- 2 cloves garlic, minced
- 1 teaspoon ground cumin
- 1 teaspoon ground ginger
- 1 teaspoon ground cinnamon
- 1/2 teaspoon ground turmeric
- 1/4 teaspoon ground cloves
- 1/4 teaspoon ground nutmeg
- 1/2 cup dried apricots, chopped
- 1/2 cup green olives
- 1 preserved lemon, thinly sliced
- 1 cup chicken broth
- Fresh cilantro for garnish

Instructions:
1. Season the chicken thighs with salt and pepper.
2. Heat olive oil in a tagine or large skillet over medium-high heat. Add the chicken thighs and brown on both sides, about 5 minutes per side. Remove the chicken and set aside.

3. In the same tagine or skillet, add thinly sliced onion and minced garlic. Cook until softened, about 5 minutes.
4. Stir in ground cumin, ground ginger, ground cinnamon, ground turmeric, ground cloves, and ground nutmeg. Cook for another minute until fragrant.
5. Return the browned chicken thighs to the tagine or skillet. Add chopped dried apricots, green olives, and thinly sliced preserved lemon.
6. Pour chicken broth over the chicken and bring to a simmer.
7. Cover and simmer over low heat for 45 minutes to 1 hour, until the chicken is tender and cooked through.
8. Garnish with fresh cilantro before serving.

Serving Suggestion: Moroccan Chicken Tagine is traditionally served with couscous or crusty bread to soak up the flavorful sauce. Serve with a side of Moroccan-style roasted vegetables or a simple salad for a complete meal.

Recipe 8: Chinese General Tso's Chicken

Preparation Time: 15 minutes
Cooking Time: 15 minutes
Total Time: 30 minutes
Servings: 4

Ingredients:
- 1 lb boneless, skinless chicken thighs, cut into bite-sized pieces
- Salt and pepper to taste
- 1/2 cup cornstarch
- 2 tablespoons vegetable oil, for frying
- 3 cloves garlic, minced
- 1 tablespoon fresh ginger, minced
- 2 green onions, sliced
- 1/2 cup chicken broth
- 2 tablespoons soy sauce
- 2 tablespoons hoisin sauce
- 2 tablespoons rice vinegar
- 2 tablespoons granulated sugar
- 1 tablespoon cornstarch mixed with 2 tablespoons water (cornstarch slurry)
- Sesame seeds for garnish
- Sliced green onions for garnish

Instructions:
1. Season the chicken pieces with salt and pepper. Coat them evenly with cornstarch.
2. Heat vegetable oil in a large skillet or wok over medium-high heat. Fry the coated chicken pieces in batches until golden and crispy, about 3-4 minutes per side. Remove and drain on paper towels.

3. In the same skillet or wok, remove excess oil, leaving about 1 tablespoon behind. Add minced garlic, minced ginger, and sliced green onions. Stir-fry for 1-2 minutes until fragrant.
4. Pour in chicken broth, soy sauce, hoisin sauce, rice vinegar, and granulated sugar. Bring to a simmer.
5. Stir in the cornstarch slurry and cook until the sauce thickens, about 1-2 minutes.
6. Return the fried chicken pieces to the skillet or wok. Toss to coat evenly with the sauce.
7. Remove from heat and transfer to a serving plate.
8. Garnish with sesame seeds and sliced green onions before serving.

Serving Suggestion: Serve General Tso's Chicken hot over steamed white rice. Pair with steamed broccoli or stir-fried vegetables for a classic Chinese takeout-inspired meal.

Recipe 9: Greek Chicken Souvlaki

Preparation Time: 20 minutes (plus marinating time)
Cooking Time: 10 minutes
Total Time: 30 minutes (plus marinating time)
Servings: 4

Ingredients:
- 1 lb boneless, skinless chicken breasts, cut into cubes
- Salt and pepper to taste
- 1/4 cup olive oil
- 2 tablespoons fresh lemon juice
- 2 cloves garlic, minced

- 1 teaspoon dried oregano
- 1/2 teaspoon dried thyme
- 1/2 teaspoon dried rosemary
- 1/2 teaspoon paprika
- 1/4 teaspoon cayenne pepper (optional)
- Wooden skewers, soaked in water for at least 30 minutes
- Tzatziki sauce for serving
- Pita bread for serving
- Sliced tomatoes, cucumbers, and red onions for serving

Instructions:
1. Season the chicken cubes with salt and pepper.
2. In a bowl, whisk together olive oil, fresh lemon juice, minced garlic, dried oregano, dried thyme, dried rosemary, paprika, and cayenne pepper (if using). Add the seasoned chicken cubes and toss to coat. Cover and marinate in the refrigerator for at least 1 hour, or overnight for best results.
3. Preheat grill or grill pan over medium-high heat.
4. Thread marinated chicken cubes onto the soaked wooden skewers.
5. Grill the chicken skewers for 3-4 minutes on each side, or until cooked through and slightly charred.
6. Remove from the grill and let rest for a few minutes.
7. Serve the Greek Chicken Souvlaki hot with tzatziki sauce, pita bread, and sliced tomatoes, cucumbers, and red onions.

Serving Suggestion: Serve the Greek Chicken Souvlaki as a traditional Greek gyro by wrapping the grilled chicken skewers in warm pita bread with sliced tomatoes, cucumbers, red onions, and tzatziki sauce.

Pair with a Greek salad and lemon-roasted potatoes for a complete Mediterranean feast.

Recipe 10: Brazilian Chicken Feijoada

Preparation Time: 30 minutes (plus soaking time for beans)
Cooking Time: 2 hours
Total Time: 2 hours 30 minutes (plus soaking time for beans)
Servings: 6-8

Ingredients:
- 1 lb dried black beans, soaked overnight
- 1 lb boneless, skinless chicken thighs, cut into chunks
- 1/2 lb smoked sausage (linguiça or chorizo), sliced
- 1/2 lb bacon, chopped
- 1 onion, chopped
- 4 cloves garlic, minced
- 2 bay leaves
- 1 teaspoon ground cumin
- 1 teaspoon paprika
- Salt and pepper to taste
- 6 cups chicken broth
- Cooked white rice for serving
- Chopped fresh cilantro for garnish
- Orange slices for serving (optional)

Instructions:
1. Drain and rinse the soaked black beans. Set aside.
2. In a large Dutch oven or heavy-bottomed pot, cook the chopped bacon over medium heat until crispy.

Remove the bacon and set aside, leaving the rendered fat in the pot.
3. Add sliced smoked sausage to the pot and cook until browned, about 5 minutes. Remove and set aside.
4. In the same pot, add chopped onion and minced garlic. Cook until softened, about 5 minutes.
5. Stir in the soaked black beans, chicken chunks, cooked bacon, cooked sausage, bay leaves, ground cumin, paprika, salt, and pepper.
6. Pour in chicken broth and bring to a boil. Reduce heat to low, cover, and simmer for 1.5 to 2 hours, stirring occasionally, until the beans are tender and the chicken is cooked through.
7. Remove the bay leaves and discard.
8. Serve the Brazilian Chicken Feijoada hot over cooked white rice, garnished with chopped fresh cilantro. Serve with orange slices on the side for squeezing over the dish, if desired.

Serving Suggestion: Brazilian Chicken Feijoada is traditionally served with farofa (toasted cassava flour), sliced oranges, and collard greens sautéed with garlic. Enjoy with a caipirinha (Brazilian cocktail) for a true taste of Brazil.

Recipe 11: Spanish Chicken Paella

Preparation Time: 15 minutes
Cooking Time: 40 minutes
Total Time: 55 minutes
Servings: 4

Ingredients:
- 1 lb chicken thighs, bone-in and skin-on, cut into pieces
- Salt and pepper to taste
- 2 tablespoons olive oil
- 1 onion, chopped
- 2 cloves garlic, minced
- 1 red bell pepper, sliced
- 1 yellow bell pepper, sliced
- 1 cup Arborio rice
- 1 pinch saffron threads
- 2 cups chicken broth
- 1 cup canned diced tomatoes
- 1/2 cup frozen peas
- 1 lemon, cut into wedges
- Fresh parsley for garnish

Instructions:
1. Season the chicken thighs with salt and pepper.
2. Heat olive oil in a large skillet or paella pan over medium-high heat. Add the chicken thighs and cook until browned on all sides, about 5 minutes. Remove and set aside.
3. In the same skillet or paella pan, add chopped onion, minced garlic, and sliced bell peppers. Cook until softened, about 5 minutes.

4. Stir in Arborio rice and saffron threads, toasting for 1-2 minutes until fragrant.
5. Pour in chicken broth and canned diced tomatoes. Bring to a simmer.
6. Return the browned chicken thighs to the skillet or paella pan, nestling them into the rice mixture. Cover and simmer over low heat for 20-25 minutes, or until the rice is cooked and the chicken is tender.
7. Sprinkle frozen peas over the top and cook for an additional 5 minutes until heated through.
8. Garnish with lemon wedges and fresh parsley before serving.

Serving Suggestion: Serve the Spanish Chicken Paella hot, straight from the skillet or paella pan, garnished with fresh parsley and lemon wedges. Pair with a crisp green salad dressed with lemon vinaigrette for a refreshing contrast.

Recipe 12: Jamaican Jerk Chicken

Preparation Time: 20 minutes (plus marinating time)
Cooking Time: 25 minutes
Total Time: 45 minutes (plus marinating time)
Servings: 4

Ingredients:
- 4 chicken leg quarters (drumsticks and thighs), skin-on
- Salt and pepper to taste
- 1/4 cup soy sauce
- 1/4 cup lime juice
- 2 tablespoons olive oil
- 2 tablespoons brown sugar
- 4 cloves garlic, minced
- 2 tablespoons fresh ginger, grated
- 2 tablespoons Jamaican jerk seasoning
- 1 teaspoon dried thyme
- 1 teaspoon ground allspice
- 1/2 teaspoon ground cinnamon
- 1/2 teaspoon ground nutmeg
- 1/2 teaspoon cayenne pepper (adjust to taste)
- Sliced green onions and lime wedges for garnish

Instructions:
1. Season the chicken leg quarters with salt and pepper.
2. In a bowl, whisk together soy sauce, lime juice, olive oil, brown sugar, minced garlic, grated ginger, Jamaican jerk seasoning, dried thyme, ground allspice, ground cinnamon, ground nutmeg, and cayenne pepper.

3. Place the seasoned chicken leg quarters in a large resealable plastic bag. Pour the marinade over the chicken, seal the bag, and massage to coat the chicken evenly. Marinate in the refrigerator for at least 4 hours, or overnight for best results.
4. Preheat grill to medium-high heat.
5. Remove the chicken from the marinade and discard the excess marinade.
6. Grill the chicken leg quarters for 10-12 minutes per side, or until cooked through and charred on the outside. The internal temperature should reach 165°F (75°C).
7. Remove from the grill and let rest for a few minutes before serving.
8. Garnish with sliced green onions and lime wedges before serving.

Serving Suggestion: Serve the Jamaican Jerk Chicken hot with traditional Jamaican rice and peas, along with fried plantains or grilled pineapple slices. Pair with a refreshing Jamaican sorrel drink or coconut water for a taste of the Caribbean.

Recipe 13: Korean Fried Chicken (Yangnyeom Chicken)

Preparation Time: 20 minutes (plus marinating time)
Cooking Time: 20 minutes
Total Time: 40 minutes (plus marinating time)
Servings: 4

Ingredients:
- 2 lbs chicken wings, separated into drumettes and flats
- Salt and pepper to taste
- 1 cup cornstarch
- Vegetable oil, for frying
- 1/2 cup gochujang (Korean red chili paste)
- 1/4 cup soy sauce
- 1/4 cup rice vinegar
- 1/4 cup honey
- 2 tablespoons sesame oil
- 4 cloves garlic, minced
- 2 teaspoons grated fresh ginger
- 1 tablespoon toasted sesame seeds
- Sliced green onions for garnish

Instructions:
1. Season the chicken wings with salt and pepper.
2. Coat the chicken wings evenly with cornstarch, shaking off any excess.
3. Heat vegetable oil in a large skillet or deep fryer to 350°F (175°C).
4. In batches, fry the coated chicken wings until golden and crispy, about 8-10 minutes per batch. Drain on paper towels.
5. In a separate bowl, whisk together gochujang, soy sauce, rice vinegar, honey, sesame oil, minced garlic, and grated ginger to make the sauce.

6. Transfer the fried chicken wings to a large bowl.
Pour the sauce over the wings and toss to coat evenly.
7. Garnish with toasted sesame seeds and sliced green
onions before serving.

Serving Suggestion: Serve the Korean Fried Chicken
hot with steamed white rice and pickled radishes.
Enjoy with ice-cold beer or soju for an authentic
Korean pub experience.

Recipe 14: Lebanese Chicken Shawarma

Preparation Time: 20 minutes (plus marinating time)
Cooking Time: 25 minutes
Total Time: 45 minutes (plus marinating time)
Servings: 4

Ingredients:
- 1 lb boneless, skinless chicken thighs, thinly sliced
- Salt and pepper to taste
- 2 tablespoons olive oil
- 2 tablespoons plain yogurt
- 2 tablespoons lemon juice
- 2 cloves garlic, minced
- 1 teaspoon ground cumin
- 1 teaspoon ground coriander
- 1/2 teaspoon paprika
- 1/2 teaspoon ground turmeric
- 1/4 teaspoon ground cinnamon
- 1/4 teaspoon cayenne pepper (adjust to taste)
- Pita bread for serving
- Sliced tomatoes, cucumbers, and red onions for serving
- Tahini sauce or garlic sauce for serving
- Fresh parsley for garnish

Instructions:
1. Season the chicken thighs with salt and pepper.
2. In a bowl, whisk together olive oil, plain yogurt, lemon juice, minced garlic, ground cumin, ground coriander, paprika, ground turmeric, ground cinnamon, and cayenne pepper.
3. Add the seasoned chicken thighs to the marinade, tossing to coat evenly. Cover and refrigerate for at least 2 hours, or overnight for best results.
4. Preheat grill or grill pan over medium-high heat.
5. Thread the marinated chicken thighs onto skewers.
6. Grill the chicken skewers for 4-5 minutes on each side, or until cooked through and lightly charred.
7. Remove from the grill and let rest for a few minutes before slicing thinly.

8. Serve the Lebanese Chicken Shawarma hot, wrapped in warm pita bread with sliced tomatoes, cucumbers, red onions, and tahini sauce or garlic sauce. Garnish with fresh parsley.

Serving Suggestion: Serve the Lebanese Chicken Shawarma as a sandwich with a side of tabbouleh salad or fattoush salad. Enjoy with a refreshing mint lemonade or ayran (yoghourt drink) for a taste of Lebanon.

Recipe 15: Turkish Chicken Kebabs (Tavuk Şiş)

Preparation Time: 20 minutes (plus marinating time)
Cooking Time: 10 minutes
Total Time: 30 minutes (plus marinating time)
Servings: 4

Ingredients:
- 1 lb chicken breast, cut into cubes

- Salt and pepper to taste
- 1/4 cup olive oil
- 2 tablespoons plain yogurt
- 2 tablespoons lemon juice
- 2 cloves garlic, minced
- 1 teaspoon ground cumin
- 1 teaspoon paprika
- 1/2 teaspoon ground turmeric
- 1/2 teaspoon ground sumac
- 1/4 teaspoon ground cinnamon
- Wooden skewers, soaked in water for at least 30 minutes
- Flatbread or pita bread for serving
- Sliced tomatoes, cucumbers, and red onions for serving
- Yogurt sauce or tahini sauce for serving
- Fresh parsley for garnish

Instructions:
1. Season the chicken cubes with salt and pepper.
2. In a bowl, whisk together olive oil, plain yogurt, lemon juice, minced garlic, ground cumin, paprika, ground turmeric, ground sumac, and ground cinnamon.
3. Add the seasoned chicken cubes to the marinade, tossing to coat evenly. Cover and refrigerate for at least 2 hours, or overnight for best results.
4. Preheat grill or grill pan over medium-high heat.
5. Thread the marinated chicken cubes onto skewers.
6. Grill the chicken kebabs for 3-4 minutes on each side, or until cooked through and lightly charred.
7. Remove from the grill and let rest for a few minutes before serving.
8. Serve the Turkish Chicken Kebabs hot, alongside flatbread or pita bread with sliced tomatoes,

cucumbers, red onions, and yogurt sauce or tahini sauce. Garnish with fresh parsley.

Serving Suggestion: Serve the Turkish Chicken Kebabs with a side of bulgur pilaf or rice pilaf. Enjoy with a glass of ayran (yogurt drink) or Turkish tea for an authentic Turkish dining experience.

Recipe 16: Vietnamese Chicken Pho

Preparation Time: 30 minutes
Cooking Time: 2 hours
Total Time: 2 hours 30 minutes
Servings: 4

Ingredients:
- 2 lbs chicken pieces (such as thighs, drumsticks, and/or breasts)

- 2 onions, halved
- 1 piece ginger (about 3 inches), halved lengthwise
- 4 cloves garlic, smashed
- 4 whole star anise
- 4 whole cloves
- 1 cinnamon stick
- 1 tablespoon coriander seeds
- 1 tablespoon sugar
- 1 tablespoon fish sauce
- 1 teaspoon salt
- 8 cups chicken broth
- 8 oz dried rice noodles
- Garnishes:
  - Fresh cilantro leaves
  - Thinly sliced green onions
  - Bean sprouts
  - Thai basil leaves
  - Lime wedges
  - Sliced jalapeños
  - Hoisin sauce
  - Sriracha sauce

Instructions:
1. In a large pot, add chicken pieces, halved onions, halved ginger, smashed garlic, star anise, cloves, cinnamon stick, coriander seeds, sugar, fish sauce, salt, and chicken broth.
2. Bring the mixture to a boil, then reduce the heat to low and simmer for 1.5 to 2 hours, skimming off any foam that rises to the surface.
3. Once the broth is flavorful and the chicken is cooked through, remove the chicken pieces and shred the meat. Set aside.
4. Strain the broth through a fine-mesh sieve, discarding the solids.

5. Return the strained broth to the pot and bring to a simmer.
6. Cook the rice noodles according to package instructions until al dente. Drain and rinse under cold water.
7. To serve, divide the cooked rice noodles among serving bowls. Top with shredded chicken and ladle hot broth over the top.
8. Serve the Vietnamese Chicken Pho hot, accompanied by a platter of garnishes including fresh cilantro leaves, thinly sliced green onions, bean sprouts, Thai basil leaves, lime wedges, sliced jalapeños, hoisin sauce, and sriracha sauce. Let diners customize their bowls with their preferred toppings.

Serving Suggestion: Vietnamese Chicken Pho is traditionally served with a side of fresh herbs, bean sprouts, lime wedges, and various sauces for added flavor. Enjoy with a cup of Vietnamese iced coffee or hot green tea for a satisfying meal.

Recipe 17: Argentinean Chicken Empanadas

Preparation Time: 30 minutes
Cooking Time: 25 minutes
Total Time: 55 minutes
Servings: 6-8

Ingredients:
For the dough:
- 3 cups all-purpose flour
- 1 teaspoon salt
- 1/2 cup unsalted butter, cold and cut into cubes

- 1/2 cup cold water
- 1 egg, beaten (for egg wash)
For the filling:
- 2 tablespoons olive oil
- 1 onion, finely chopped
- 2 cloves garlic, minced
- 1 bell pepper, diced
- 1 teaspoon ground cumin
- 1 teaspoon paprika
- 1/2 teaspoon dried oregano
- 1/2 teaspoon salt
- 1/4 teaspoon black pepper
- 2 cups cooked chicken, shredded
- 1/2 cup green olives, pitted and chopped
- 2 hard-boiled eggs, chopped
- 1/4 cup raisins (optional)
- 1/4 cup chopped fresh parsley
- Additional salt and pepper to taste

Instructions:
1. In a large bowl, whisk together flour and salt. Cut in the cold butter using a pastry cutter or your fingertips until the mixture resembles coarse crumbs.
2. Gradually add cold water, mixing until the dough comes together. Shape the dough into a ball, wrap it in plastic wrap, and refrigerate for at least 30 minutes.
3. In a skillet, heat olive oil over medium heat. Add chopped onion, minced garlic, and diced bell pepper. Cook until softened, about 5 minutes.
4. Stir in ground cumin, paprika, dried oregano, salt, and black pepper. Cook for another minute until fragrant.
5. Add shredded chicken, chopped green olives, chopped hard-boiled eggs, raisins (if using), and chopped fresh parsley. Mix well to combine. Adjust

seasoning with additional salt and pepper if needed. Remove from heat and let cool slightly.
6. Preheat oven to 375°F (190°C). Line a baking sheet with parchment paper.
7. On a lightly floured surface, roll out the chilled dough to about 1/8 inch thickness. Use a round cutter or a small bowl to cut out circles of dough.
8. Spoon a tablespoon of the chicken filling onto the center of each dough circle. Fold the dough over the filling to form a half-moon shape. Press the edges together to seal, then crimp with a fork.
9. Place the empanadas on the prepared baking sheet. Brush the tops with beaten egg for a golden finish.
10. Bake in the preheated oven for 20-25 minutes, or until golden brown and crisp.
11. Remove from the oven and let cool slightly before serving.

Serving Suggestion: Serve the Argentinean Chicken Empanadas hot, as a savory appetizer or main dish. Enjoy with chimichurri sauce or salsa criolla for dipping, along with a side of Argentinean salad or grilled vegetables. Pair with a glass of Malbec wine for an authentic Argentinean dining experience.

Recipe 18: Filipino Chicken Adobo

Preparation Time: 10 minutes
Cooking Time: 45 minutes
Total Time: 55 minutes
Servings: 4

Ingredients:
- 2 lbs chicken thighs, bone-in and skin-on
- 1/2 cup soy sauce
- 1/2 cup white vinegar
- 1 cup water
- 4 cloves garlic, minced
- 1 onion, sliced
- 2 bay leaves
- 1 teaspoon whole peppercorns
- 1 tablespoon cooking oil
- Steamed rice for serving
- Chopped green onions for garnish (optional)

Instructions:
1. In a large bowl, combine soy sauce, white vinegar, water, minced garlic, sliced onion, bay leaves, and whole peppercorns. Mix well.
2. Add the chicken thighs to the marinade, making sure they are fully submerged. Cover and refrigerate for at least 30 minutes, or overnight for best results.
3. Heat cooking oil in a large skillet or pot over medium-high heat. Remove the chicken thighs from the marinade, reserving the marinade.
4. Brown the chicken thighs on both sides until golden brown, about 5 minutes per side.
5. Pour the reserved marinade over the chicken thighs. Bring to a boil, then reduce heat to low, cover, and simmer for 30-35 minutes, stirring occasionally, until the chicken is cooked through and tender.
6. Remove the lid and continue to simmer for an additional 10 minutes to allow the sauce to reduce and thicken.

7. Serve the Filipino Chicken Adobo hot over steamed rice, spooning the sauce over the chicken. Garnish with chopped green onions, if desired.

Serving Suggestion: Serve the Filipino Chicken Adobo with a side of steamed vegetables or a fresh tomato and onion salad. Enjoy with a cold glass of iced tea or calamansi juice for a refreshing Filipino meal.

Recipe 19: Ethiopian Doro Wat

Preparation Time: 20 minutes
Cooking Time: 1 hour
Total Time: 1 hour 20 minutes
Servings: 4

Ingredients:
- 2 lbs chicken drumsticks and thighs, skin-on
- Salt to taste
- 2 tablespoons clarified butter (niter kibbeh) or regular butter
- 2 onions, finely chopped
- 4 cloves garlic, minced
- 1 tablespoon fresh ginger, grated

- 2 tablespoons berbere spice blend
- 1 teaspoon paprika
- 1/2 teaspoon ground cumin
- 1/2 teaspoon ground coriander
- 1/4 teaspoon ground cardamom
- 1/4 teaspoon ground fenugreek
- 1/4 teaspoon ground nutmeg
- 1 cup chicken broth
- 2 tablespoons tomato paste
- 4 hard-boiled eggs, peeled
- Fresh cilantro for garnish

Instructions:
1. Season the chicken drumsticks and thighs with salt.
2. In a large skillet or pot, heat clarified butter over medium heat. Add finely chopped onions and cook until softened and translucent, about 5-7 minutes.
3. Stir in minced garlic and grated ginger, cooking for another 2 minutes until fragrant.
4. Add berbere spice blend, paprika, ground cumin, ground coriander, ground cardamom, ground fenugreek, and ground nutmeg. Cook, stirring constantly, for 2-3 minutes until the spices are toasted and fragrant.
5. Place the seasoned chicken pieces in the skillet or pot, coating them with the spice mixture. Cook for 5 minutes, turning occasionally to brown on all sides.
6. Pour in chicken broth and tomato paste. Bring to a simmer, then reduce heat to low, cover, and cook for 40-45 minutes, or until the chicken is cooked through and tender.
7. Add peeled hard-boiled eggs to the pot, gently nestling them among the chicken pieces. Simmer for an additional 5-10 minutes to allow the flavors to meld.

8. Serve the Ethiopian Doro Wat hot, garnished with fresh cilantro. Enjoy with injera (Ethiopian flatbread) or steamed rice.

Serving Suggestion: Ethiopian Doro Wat is traditionally served with injera, a spongy sourdough flatbread used to scoop up the flavorful stew. Enjoy with a side of Ethiopian lentils or vegetables for a complete Ethiopian dining experience.

Recipe 20: Russian Chicken Kiev

Preparation Time: 30 minutes
Cooking Time: 15 minutes
Total Time: 45 minutes
Servings: 4

Ingredients:
- 4 boneless, skinless chicken breast halves
- Salt and pepper to taste
- 8 tablespoons unsalted butter, softened
- 2 cloves garlic, minced
- 2 tablespoons chopped fresh parsley
- 1 tablespoon chopped fresh dill
- 1 teaspoon lemon zest
- 1 cup all-purpose flour
- 2 eggs, beaten
- 1 cup breadcrumbs

- Vegetable oil for frying
- Lemon wedges for serving

Instructions:
1. Place each chicken breast half between two sheets of plastic wrap. Pound with a meat mallet or rolling pin until about 1/4 inch thick. Season both sides with salt and pepper.
2. In a small bowl, mix together softened butter, minced garlic, chopped fresh parsley, chopped fresh dill, and lemon zest until well combined.
3. Spoon about 2 tablespoons of the herb butter mixture onto the center of each flattened chicken breast. Fold the sides of the chicken over the butter to enclose it, then roll up tightly into a cylinder shape. Secure with toothpicks if needed. Repeat with the remaining chicken breasts and butter mixture.
4. Place flour, beaten eggs, and breadcrumbs in separate shallow dishes.
5. Dredge each chicken roll in flour, shaking off any excess. Dip into beaten eggs, then coat evenly with breadcrumbs, pressing gently to adhere.
6. Heat vegetable oil in a large skillet over medium-high heat. Carefully add the breaded chicken rolls to the hot oil and fry until golden brown and cooked through, about 6-7 minutes per side.
7. Remove the chicken Kiev from the skillet and drain on paper towels.
8. Remove the toothpicks before serving. Serve the Russian Chicken Kiev hot with lemon wedges on the side.

Serving Suggestion: Serve the Russian Chicken Kiev with a side of mashed potatoes or buttered noodles and steamed vegetables. Enjoy with a glass of chilled

vodka or sparkling water with lemon for a classic
Russian meal.

Recipe 21: Thai Green Curry Chicken

Preparation Time: 15 minutes
Cooking Time: 20 minutes
Total Time: 35 minutes
Servings: 4

Ingredients:
- 1 lb boneless, skinless chicken breasts or thighs, cut
into bite-sized pieces
- Salt and pepper to taste
- 2 tablespoons vegetable oil
- 3 tablespoons green curry paste
- 1 can (13.5 oz) coconut milk
- 1 cup chicken broth
- 1 tablespoon fish sauce
- 1 tablespoon palm sugar or brown sugar
- 1 red bell pepper, sliced
- 1 green bell pepper, sliced

- 1 zucchini, sliced
- 1 cup bamboo shoots (optional)
- 1 cup Thai basil leaves
- Cooked rice for serving

Instructions:
1. Season the chicken pieces with salt and pepper.
2. Heat vegetable oil in a large skillet or wok over medium-high heat. Add green curry paste and cook for 1-2 minutes, stirring constantly, until fragrant.
3. Stir in coconut milk, chicken broth, fish sauce, and palm sugar. Bring to a simmer.
4. Add the sliced chicken to the skillet or wok, stirring to coat with the curry sauce. Cook for 5 minutes.
5. Add sliced red bell pepper, green bell pepper, zucchini, and bamboo shoots (if using) to the skillet or wok. Simmer for another 10 minutes, or until the vegetables are tender and the chicken is cooked through.
6. Stir in Thai basil leaves and cook for an additional minute until wilted.
7. Remove from heat and serve the Thai Green Curry Chicken hot over cooked rice.

Serving Suggestion: Thai Green Curry Chicken is traditionally served with steamed jasmine rice or Thai sticky rice. Garnish with additional Thai basil leaves and sliced red chili peppers for extra heat if desired. Enjoy with a side of Thai cucumber salad or stir-fried vegetables.

Recipe 22: Cuban Chicken Mojo

Preparation Time: 15 minutes
Cooking Time: 30 minutes
Total Time: 45 minutes
Servings: 4

Ingredients:
- 4 bone-in, skin-on chicken thighs
- Salt and pepper to taste
- 1/4 cup olive oil
- 1/4 cup orange juice
- 1/4 cup lime juice
- 4 cloves garlic, minced
- 1 teaspoon ground cumin
- 1 teaspoon dried oregano
- 1 teaspoon paprika
- 1/2 teaspoon red pepper flakes (adjust to taste)
- Chopped fresh cilantro for garnish
- Lime wedges for serving

Instructions:
1. Season the chicken thighs with salt and pepper.
2. In a large bowl, whisk together olive oil, orange juice, lime juice, minced garlic, ground cumin, dried oregano, paprika, and red pepper flakes.
3. Add the seasoned chicken thighs to the marinade, tossing to coat evenly. Cover and refrigerate for at least 1 hour, or overnight for best results.
4. Preheat oven to 375°F (190°C).
5. Remove the chicken thighs from the marinade and place them in a baking dish or cast-iron skillet.
6. Bake in the preheated oven for 25-30 minutes, or until the chicken is cooked through and golden brown, basting occasionally with the marinade.

7. Remove from the oven and let rest for a few minutes before serving.
8. Serve the Cuban Chicken Mojo hot, garnished with chopped fresh cilantro and lime wedges on the side.

Serving Suggestion: Serve the Cuban Chicken Mojo with a side of black beans and rice or yuca con mojo (yucca with garlic sauce). Enjoy with a cold glass of mojito or Cuba libre for a taste of Cuba.

Recipe 23: Pakistani Chicken Biryani

Preparation Time: 30 minutes (plus marinating time)
Cooking Time: 1 hour
Total Time: 1 hour 30 minutes (plus marinating time)
Servings: 6

Ingredients:
For the chicken marinade:
- 2 lbs chicken thighs, bone-in and skin-on, cut into pieces
- 1 cup plain yogurt
- 2 tablespoons ginger garlic paste
- 1 teaspoon ground cumin
- 1 teaspoon ground coriander
- 1 teaspoon chili powder
- 1/2 teaspoon ground turmeric
- Salt to taste
- Freshly squeezed lemon juice from 1 lemon

- Fresh cilantro and mint leaves, chopped for garnish
For the rice:
- 3 cups basmati rice, soaked for 30 minutes and drained
- 4 cups water
- 2 bay leaves
- 4 whole cloves
- 4 whole green cardamom pods
- 2-inch cinnamon stick
- Salt to taste
- 1 tablespoon ghee or clarified butter
For assembling:
- 2 large onions, thinly sliced and fried until golden brown
- Saffron strands soaked in 1/4 cup warm milk
- Ghee or clarified butter for drizzling

Instructions:
1. In a large bowl, combine plain yogurt, ginger garlic paste, ground cumin, ground coriander, chili powder, ground turmeric, salt, and freshly squeezed lemon juice to make the marinade.
2. Add the chicken pieces to the marinade, tossing to coat evenly. Cover and refrigerate for at least 4 hours, or overnight for best results.
3. In a large pot, bring water to a boil. Add soaked and drained basmati rice, bay leaves, whole cloves, whole green cardamom pods, cinnamon stick, salt, and ghee. Stir gently and cook until the rice is 70% cooked. Drain and set aside.
4. Preheat oven to 350°F (175°C).
5. In a large ovenproof dish, spread a layer of cooked rice evenly at the bottom.
6. Arrange the marinated chicken pieces over the rice in an even layer.

7. Sprinkle fried onions over the chicken layer.
8. Spread the remaining cooked rice over the chicken and fried onions.
9. Drizzle saffron-infused milk over the rice.
10. Dot the top layer of rice with ghee or clarified butter.
11. Cover the dish tightly with aluminum foil and bake in the preheated oven for 30-40 minutes, or until the chicken is cooked through and the rice is fully cooked.
12. Remove from the oven and let rest for a few minutes before serving.
13. Garnish the Pakistani Chicken Biryani with chopped fresh cilantro and mint leaves before serving.

Serving Suggestion: Serve the Pakistani Chicken Biryani hot, garnished with additional fried onions and served with raita (yogurt sauce), sliced cucumbers, and tomatoes on the side. Enjoy with mango chutney and papadum for a complete Pakistani feast.

Recipe 24: Malaysian Chicken Satay

Preparation Time: 30 minutes (plus marinating time)
Cooking Time: 10 minutes
Total Time: 40 minutes (plus marinating time)
Servings: 4

Ingredients:
For the chicken marinade:
- 1 lb chicken breast or thigh meat, cut into thin strips
- 2 tablespoons soy sauce
- 2 tablespoons vegetable oil

- 2 cloves garlic, minced
- 1 tablespoon brown sugar
- 1 teaspoon ground coriander
- 1/2 teaspoon ground cumin
- 1/2 teaspoon turmeric powder
- Salt to taste

For the peanut sauce:
- 1/2 cup creamy peanut butter
- 1/4 cup coconut milk
- 2 tablespoons soy sauce
- 1 tablespoon brown sugar
- 1 tablespoon lime juice
- 1 teaspoon chili garlic sauce (optional)
- Water (as needed to adjust consistency)

For serving:
- Bamboo skewers, soaked in water for at least 30 minutes
- Sliced cucumbers and onions for garnish
- Fresh cilantro leaves for garnish

Instructions:
1. In a bowl, combine soy sauce, vegetable oil, minced garlic, brown sugar, ground coriander, ground cumin, turmeric powder, and salt to make the marinade.
2. Add the chicken strips to the marinade, tossing to coat evenly. Cover and refrigerate for at least 2 hours, or overnight for best results.
3. Preheat grill or grill pan over medium-high heat.
4. Thread the marinated chicken strips onto soaked bamboo skewers.
5. Grill the chicken satay skewers for 3-4 minutes on each side, or until cooked through and slightly charred.
6. In the meantime, prepare the peanut sauce. In a small saucepan, combine creamy peanut butter,

coconut milk, soy sauce, brown sugar, lime juice, and chili garlic sauce (if using). Cook over low heat, stirring constantly, until the sauce is smooth and heated through. If the sauce is too thick, thin it out with water until desired consistency is reached.
7. Serve the grilled Malaysian Chicken Satay hot with peanut sauce on the side for dipping.
8. Garnish with sliced cucumbers, onions, and fresh cilantro leaves.

Serving Suggestion: Malaysian Chicken Satay is traditionally served with a side of compressed rice cakes (ketupat) or steamed jasmine rice. Enjoy with a refreshing Malaysian fruit juice or iced tea for a delightful Malaysian street food experience.

Recipe 25: Italian Chicken Piccata

Preparation Time: 15 minutes
Cooking Time: 15 minutes
Total Time: 30 minutes
Servings: 4

Ingredients:
- 4 boneless, skinless chicken breasts
- Salt and pepper to taste
- 1/2 cup all-purpose flour
- 2 tablespoons olive oil
- 4 tablespoons unsalted butter
- 1/2 cup chicken broth
- 1/4 cup freshly squeezed lemon juice
- 1/4 cup capers, drained
- 2 tablespoons chopped fresh parsley

- Lemon slices for garnish

Instructions:
1. Place each chicken breast between two sheets of plastic wrap. Pound with a meat mallet or rolling pin until about 1/4 inch thick. Season both sides with salt and pepper.
2. Dredge the seasoned chicken breasts in flour, shaking off any excess.
3. In a large skillet, heat olive oil over medium-high heat. Add 2 tablespoons of unsalted butter to the skillet.
4. Add the floured chicken breasts to the skillet and cook for 3-4 minutes on each side, or until golden brown and cooked through. Remove from the skillet and transfer to a plate. Cover with foil to keep warm.
5. In the same skillet, add chicken broth and freshly squeezed lemon juice, scraping up any browned bits from the bottom of the skillet.
6. Bring the sauce to a simmer and cook for 2-3 minutes, or until slightly reduced.
7. Stir in drained capers and remaining 2 tablespoons of unsalted butter until melted and incorporated into the sauce.
8. Return the cooked chicken breasts to the skillet, turning to coat them in the lemon caper sauce.
9. Sprinkle chopped fresh parsley over the chicken breasts.
10. Serve the Italian Chicken Piccata hot, garnished with lemon slices.

Serving Suggestion: Italian Chicken Piccata is traditionally served with a side of pasta or mashed potatoes and steamed vegetables. Enjoy with a glass of chilled white wine such as Pinot Grigio or Sauvignon Blanc for a classic Italian meal experience.

Recipe 26: Greek Lemon Garlic Chicken

Preparation Time: 15 minutes
Cooking Time: 25 minutes
Total Time: 40 minutes
Servings: 4

Ingredients:
- 4 boneless, skinless chicken breasts
- Salt and pepper to taste
- 4 cloves garlic, minced
- 1 teaspoon dried oregano
- 1 teaspoon dried thyme
- 1/4 cup olive oil
- Zest and juice of 1 lemon
- 1/4 cup chopped fresh parsley
- Lemon wedges for serving

Instructions:
1. Season the chicken breasts with salt and pepper on both sides.

2. In a bowl, mix together minced garlic, dried oregano, dried thyme, olive oil, lemon zest, and lemon juice.
3. Place the seasoned chicken breasts in a shallow dish or resealable plastic bag. Pour the marinade over the chicken, making sure they are evenly coated. Cover and refrigerate for at least 30 minutes, or up to 4 hours.
4. Preheat grill or grill pan over medium-high heat.
5. Remove the chicken breasts from the marinade and discard any excess marinade.
6. Grill the chicken breasts for 6-7 minutes on each side, or until cooked through and no longer pink in the center.
7. Remove from the grill and let rest for a few minutes before slicing.
8. Serve the Greek Lemon Garlic Chicken hot, garnished with chopped fresh parsley and lemon wedges on the side.

Serving Suggestion: Serve the Greek Lemon Garlic Chicken with a side of Greek salad, roasted potatoes, or rice pilaf. Enjoy with a glass of chilled Assyrtiko wine for a taste of Greece.

Recipe 27: Japanese Chicken Katsu

Preparation Time: 15 minutes
Cooking Time: 15 minutes
Total Time: 30 minutes
Servings: 4

Ingredients:
- 4 boneless, skinless chicken breasts
- Salt and pepper to taste
- 1/2 cup all-purpose flour
- 2 eggs, beaten
- 1 cup panko breadcrumbs
- Vegetable oil for frying
- Tonkatsu sauce or Bulldog sauce for serving
- Shredded cabbage for serving
- Cooked rice for serving

Instructions:
1. Place each chicken breast between two sheets of plastic wrap. Pound with a meat mallet or rolling pin until about 1/2 inch thick. Season both sides with salt and pepper.
2. Set up a breading station with three shallow dishes: one with all-purpose flour, one with beaten eggs, and one with panko breadcrumbs.
3. Dredge each chicken breast in flour, shaking off any excess. Dip into beaten eggs, then coat evenly with panko breadcrumbs, pressing gently to adhere.
4. Heat vegetable oil in a large skillet or deep fryer to 350°F (175°C).
5. Carefully add the breaded chicken breasts to the hot oil and fry for 4-5 minutes on each side, or until golden brown and cooked through.
6. Remove from the oil and drain on paper towels.
7. Slice the chicken katsu into strips.
8. Serve the Japanese Chicken Katsu hot, accompanied by tonkatsu sauce or Bulldog sauce for dipping, shredded cabbage, and cooked rice.

Serving Suggestion: Japanese Chicken Katsu is traditionally served with shredded cabbage dressed

with tonkatsu sauce and a side of steamed rice. Enjoy
with a bowl of miso soup and green tea for a classic
Japanese meal.

Recipe 28: Indian Tandoori Chicken

Preparation Time: 15 minutes (plus marinating time)
Cooking Time: 25 minutes
Total Time: 40 minutes (plus marinating time)
Servings: 4

Ingredients:
- 4 chicken leg quarters (drumsticks and thighs)
- Salt to taste
- 1 cup plain yogurt
- 2 tablespoons ginger garlic paste
- 2 tablespoons lemon juice
- 2 tablespoons tandoori masala spice blend
- 1 teaspoon ground cumin
- 1 teaspoon ground coriander
- 1 teaspoon paprika
- 1/2 teaspoon ground turmeric
- 1/4 teaspoon cayenne pepper (optional, for extra
heat)
- Vegetable oil for grilling
- Fresh cilantro for garnish
- Lemon wedges for serving

Instructions:
1. Season the chicken leg quarters with salt.
2. In a bowl, combine plain yogurt, ginger garlic paste, lemon juice, tandoori masala spice blend, ground cumin, ground coriander, paprika, ground turmeric, and cayenne pepper (if using). Mix well to form the marinade.
3. Score the chicken leg quarters with a sharp knife to allow the marinade to penetrate.
4. Place the chicken leg quarters in a shallow dish or resealable plastic bag. Pour the marinade over the chicken, making sure they are evenly coated. Cover and refrigerate for at least 4 hours, or overnight for best results.
5. Preheat grill or grill pan over medium-high heat.
6. Remove the chicken leg quarters from the marinade and shake off any excess marinade.
7. Brush the grill grates with vegetable oil to prevent sticking. Place the chicken leg quarters on the grill and cook for 10-12 minutes on each side, or until charred and cooked through. The internal temperature should reach 165°F (74°C).
8. Remove from the grill and let rest for a few minutes before serving.
9. Serve the Indian Tandoori Chicken hot, garnished with fresh cilantro and lemon wedges on the side.

Serving Suggestion: Indian Tandoori Chicken is traditionally served with naan bread, basmati rice, and cucumber raita. Enjoy with a refreshing mango lassi or Indian beer for a delicious Indian feast.

Recipe 29: Spanish Chicken with Chorizo

Preparation Time: 15 minutes
Cooking Time: 30 minutes
Total Time: 45 minutes
Servings: 4

Ingredients:
- 4 bone-in, skin-on chicken thighs
- Salt and pepper to taste
- 1 tablespoon olive oil
- 4 oz Spanish chorizo sausage, sliced
- 1 onion, diced
- 2 cloves garlic, minced
- 1 red bell pepper, diced
- 1 yellow bell pepper, diced
- 1 teaspoon smoked paprika
- 1/2 teaspoon dried oregano
- 1/2 teaspoon dried thyme
- 1/2 cup dry white wine
- 1 can (14.5 oz) diced tomatoes
- 1/4 cup chopped fresh parsley

Instructions:
1. Season the chicken thighs with salt and pepper on both sides.
2. Heat olive oil in a large skillet or Dutch oven over medium-high heat. Add the chicken thighs, skin side down, and cook until golden brown, about 5 minutes per side. Remove from the skillet and set aside.
3. In the same skillet, add Spanish chorizo sausage slices and cook until slightly browned, about 2-3 minutes. Remove from the skillet and set aside.

4. Add diced onion to the skillet and cook until softened, about 3-4 minutes.
5. Stir in minced garlic, diced red bell pepper, and diced yellow bell pepper. Cook for another 2 minutes.
6. Add smoked paprika, dried oregano, and dried thyme to the skillet, stirring to coat the vegetables.
7. Pour dry white wine into the skillet, scraping up any browned bits from the bottom. Cook for 2-3 minutes to reduce slightly.
8. Stir in diced tomatoes and bring to a simmer.
9. Return the browned chicken thighs and cooked chorizo sausage slices to the skillet, nestling them into the tomato mixture.
10. Cover and simmer for 20-25 minutes, or until the chicken is cooked through and tender.
11. Garnish the Spanish Chicken with Chorizo with chopped fresh parsley before serving.

Serving Suggestion: Spanish Chicken with Chorizo is traditionally served with crusty bread or Spanish rice. Enjoy with a glass of Spanish red wine such as Rioja or Tempranillo for a taste of Spain.

Recipe 30: French Chicken Provencal

Preparation Time: 15 minutes
Cooking Time: 30 minutes
Total Time: 45 minutes
Servings: 4

Ingredients:
- 4 bone-in, skin-on chicken thighs

- Salt and pepper to taste
- 2 tablespoons olive oil
- 4 cloves garlic, minced
- 1 onion, thinly sliced
- 1 red bell pepper, sliced
- 1 yellow bell pepper, sliced
- 1 can (14.5 oz) diced tomatoes
- 1/2 cup pitted black olives
- 2 tablespoons capers, drained
- 1 teaspoon dried thyme
- 1 teaspoon dried oregano
- 1/2 teaspoon dried rosemary
- 1/2 cup dry white wine
- Fresh parsley for garnish

Instructions:
1. Season the chicken thighs with salt and pepper on both sides.
2. Heat olive oil in a large skillet or Dutch oven over medium-high heat. Add the chicken thighs, skin side down, and cook until golden brown, about 5 minutes per side. Remove from the skillet and set aside.
3. In the same skillet, add minced garlic and thinly sliced onion. Cook until softened, about 3-4 minutes.
4. Stir in sliced red bell pepper and sliced yellow bell pepper. Cook for another 2 minutes.
5. Add diced tomatoes (with their juices), pitted black olives, drained capers, dried thyme, dried oregano, and dried rosemary to the skillet, stirring to combine.
6. Pour dry white wine into the skillet and bring to a simmer.
7. Return the browned chicken thighs to the skillet, nestling them into the tomato mixture.
8. Cover and simmer for 20-25 minutes, or until the chicken is cooked through and tender.

9. Garnish the French Chicken Provencal with chopped fresh parsley before serving.

Serving Suggestion: French Chicken Provencal is traditionally served with crusty French bread or over pasta. Enjoy with a glass of French rosé wine such as Côtes de Provence for a taste of the Provence region.

Recipe 31: Korean Chicken Bulgogi

Preparation Time: 15 minutes (plus marinating time)
Cooking Time: 10 minutes
Total Time: 25 minutes (plus marinating time)
Servings: 4

Ingredients:
- 1 lb boneless, skinless chicken thighs, thinly sliced
- 2 tablespoons soy sauce
- 2 tablespoons brown sugar
- 1 tablespoon sesame oil
- 1 tablespoon rice vinegar
- 2 cloves garlic, minced
- 1 teaspoon grated fresh ginger
- 1 green onion, thinly sliced
- 1 tablespoon toasted sesame seeds
- Vegetable oil for cooking
- Cooked rice for serving
- Kimchi for serving (optional)

Instructions:
1. In a bowl, combine soy sauce, brown sugar, sesame oil, rice vinegar, minced garlic, grated fresh ginger,

sliced green onion, and toasted sesame seeds to make the marinade.
2. Add the thinly sliced chicken thighs to the marinade, tossing to coat evenly. Cover and refrigerate for at least 1 hour, or up to 4 hours.
3. Heat vegetable oil in a large skillet or wok over medium-high heat.
4. Add the marinated chicken thighs to the hot skillet in a single layer, reserving any excess marinade.
5. Cook the chicken thighs for 3-4 minutes, stirring occasionally, until browned and cooked through.
6. Pour the reserved marinade into the skillet and cook for an additional 2-3 minutes, stirring constantly, until the sauce thickens and coats the chicken.
7. Remove from heat and garnish with additional sliced green onions and toasted sesame seeds if desired.
8. Serve the Korean Chicken Bulgogi hot over cooked rice.

Serving Suggestion: Korean Chicken Bulgogi is traditionally served with steamed rice and kimchi. Enjoy with a side of Korean pickled vegetables and a bowl of hot soup for a complete Korean meal experience.

Recipe 32: Brazilian Chicken Coxinha

Preparation Time: 30 minutes
Cooking Time: 30 minutes
Total Time: 1 hour
Servings: 8

Ingredients:
For the chicken filling:
- 1 lb boneless, skinless chicken breast
- 1 onion, chopped
- 2 cloves garlic, minced
- 1 tablespoon olive oil
- Salt and pepper to taste
- 1 cup chicken broth
- 1 bay leaf
- 1/4 cup chopped fresh parsley
For the dough:
- 2 cups chicken broth
- 2 tablespoons unsalted butter
- 2 cups all-purpose flour
- 1 teaspoon salt
- 2 eggs
- 1 cup breadcrumbs
- Vegetable oil for frying

Instructions:
1. To prepare the chicken filling, heat olive oil in a skillet over medium heat. Add chopped onion and minced garlic, cooking until softened.
2. Add the chicken breast, season with salt and pepper, and cook until browned on all sides.
3. Pour in chicken broth, add a bay leaf, and bring to a simmer. Cook until the chicken is cooked through and tender, about 15-20 minutes.
4. Remove the chicken from the skillet, shred it using two forks, and return it to the skillet. Stir in chopped fresh parsley. Remove from heat and set aside.
5. To prepare the dough, in a saucepan, bring chicken broth and unsalted butter to a boil.

6. Reduce heat to low and add all-purpose flour and salt, stirring continuously until a smooth dough forms and pulls away from the sides of the pan.
7. Remove from heat and let the dough cool slightly. Once cool enough to handle, knead the dough until smooth.
8. Take a small portion of the dough, flatten it in your palm, and place a spoonful of the chicken filling in the center. Enclose the filling with the dough, shaping it into a teardrop or drumstick-like shape.
9. Beat the eggs in a bowl. Dip each coxinha into the beaten eggs, then roll it in breadcrumbs to coat evenly.
10. Heat vegetable oil in a deep fryer or large skillet over medium-high heat. Fry the coxinhas in batches until golden brown and crispy, about 4-5 minutes per batch.
11. Remove the coxinhas from the oil and drain on paper towels.
12. Serve the Brazilian Chicken Coxinha hot as a delicious appetizer or snack.

Serving Suggestion: Brazilian Chicken Coxinha is traditionally served as a snack or appetizer, accompanied by hot sauce or salsa. Enjoy with a refreshing Caipirinha cocktail for an authentic Brazilian experience.

Recipe 33: Mexican Chicken Mole

Preparation Time: 20 minutes
Cooking Time: 1 hour
Total Time: 1 hour 20 minutes

Servings: 6

Ingredients:
- 3 lbs chicken pieces (such as thighs and drumsticks), skin-on
- Salt and pepper to taste
- 2 tablespoons vegetable oil
- 1 onion, chopped
- 4 cloves garlic, minced
- 2 dried ancho chilies, stemmed and seeded
- 2 dried guajillo chilies, stemmed and seeded
- 2 cups chicken broth
- 1 can (14.5 oz) diced tomatoes
- 1/4 cup raisins
- 1/4 cup slivered almonds
- 2 tablespoons sesame seeds
- 1 tablespoon unsweetened cocoa powder
- 1 teaspoon ground cinnamon
- 1/2 teaspoon ground cumin
- 1/4 teaspoon ground cloves
- 1/4 teaspoon ground coriander
- 1/4 teaspoon ground nutmeg
- 2 tablespoons peanut butter
- 2 oz unsweetened chocolate, chopped
- 2 tablespoons sugar (optional, to taste)
- Cooked rice for serving
- Fresh cilantro for garnish

Instructions:
1. Season the chicken pieces with salt and pepper on both sides.
2. Heat vegetable oil in a large Dutch oven or heavy-bottomed pot over medium-high heat. Add the chicken pieces in batches and cook until browned on all sides. Remove from the pot and set aside.

3. In the same pot, add chopped onion and minced garlic. Cook until softened and fragrant, about 3-4 minutes.
4. Meanwhile, in a dry skillet over medium heat, toast the dried ancho chilies and guajillo chilies until fragrant, about 1-2 minutes per side. Remove from heat and transfer to a bowl. Cover with hot water and let soak for 15-20 minutes to soften.
5. In a blender or food processor, combine the soaked chilies (drained), chicken broth, diced tomatoes, raisins, slivered almonds, sesame seeds, unsweetened cocoa powder, ground cinnamon, ground cumin, ground cloves, ground coriander, and ground nutmeg. Blend until smooth.
6. Pour the chili mixture into the pot with the cooked onions and garlic. Stir in peanut butter and chopped unsweetened chocolate until melted and incorporated.
7. Return the browned chicken pieces to the pot, along with any accumulated juices. Bring the mixture to a simmer.
8. Cover the pot and simmer gently over low heat for 45-60 minutes, stirring occasionally, until the chicken is cooked through and tender, and the sauce has thickened.
9. Taste the sauce and adjust seasoning with salt, pepper, and sugar (if using), to balance flavors.
10. Serve the Mexican Chicken Mole hot over cooked rice, garnished with fresh cilantro.

Serving Suggestion: Mexican Chicken Mole is traditionally served with rice and warm tortillas. Enjoy with a side of refried beans and Mexican-style corn for a festive and flavorful meal.

Recipe 34: Moroccan Chicken Bastilla

Preparation Time: 30 minutes
Cooking Time: 1 hour
Total Time: 1 hour 30 minutes
Servings: 6

Ingredients:
For the chicken filling:
- 2 lbs boneless, skinless chicken thighs
- Salt and pepper to taste
- 2 tablespoons olive oil
- 1 onion, finely chopped
- 2 cloves garlic, minced
- 1 teaspoon ground ginger
- 1 teaspoon ground cinnamon
- 1/2 teaspoon ground turmeric
- 1/2 teaspoon ground cumin
- 1/4 teaspoon ground cloves
- 1/4 teaspoon ground nutmeg
- 1/4 teaspoon saffron threads, soaked in 2 tablespoons warm water
- 1/2 cup chopped fresh cilantro
- 1/2 cup chopped fresh parsley
- 1/4 cup chopped almonds
- 1/4 cup chopped dried apricots
- 1/4 cup golden raisins
- 1/4 cup pomegranate seeds (optional)
- 6 eggs, beaten
- Filo pastry sheets
- Butter, melted, for brushing
- Powdered sugar for dusting
- Ground cinnamon for dusting

Instructions:
1. Season the chicken thighs with salt and pepper on both sides.
2. Heat olive oil in a large skillet or Dutch oven over medium-high heat. Add the chicken thighs and cook until browned on both sides. Remove from the skillet and set aside.
3. In the same skillet, add finely chopped onion and minced garlic. Cook until softened and translucent.
4. Stir in ground ginger, ground cinnamon, ground turmeric, ground cumin, ground cloves, and ground nutmeg. Cook for another minute until fragrant.
5. Return the browned chicken thighs to the skillet. Pour in the saffron-infused water and bring to a simmer.
6. Cover the skillet and cook over low heat for 30-40 minutes, or until the chicken is cooked through and tender. Remove the chicken from the skillet and let cool slightly. Shred the chicken into bite-sized pieces.
7. Return the shredded chicken to the skillet. Stir in chopped fresh cilantro, chopped fresh parsley, chopped almonds, chopped dried apricots, golden raisins, and beaten eggs. Cook, stirring constantly, until the eggs are set and the mixture is thickened.
8. Preheat the oven to 375°F (190°C). Lightly grease a pie dish or baking dish.
9. Lay a filo pastry sheet in the prepared dish, allowing the edges to overhang. Brush the pastry sheet with melted butter. Repeat layering with remaining filo sheets, brushing each layer with melted butter.
10. Spoon the chicken filling over the layered filo pastry sheets. Fold the overhanging edges of filo pastry over the filling to enclose it completely.

11. Brush the top of the pastry with melted butter. Bake in the preheated oven for 25-30 minutes, or until the pastry is golden brown and crispy.
12. Remove from the oven and let cool slightly before slicing.
13. Dust the Moroccan Chicken Bastilla with powdered sugar and ground cinnamon before serving.

Serving Suggestion: Moroccan Chicken Bastilla is traditionally served as a savory-sweet dish, dusted with powdered sugar and ground cinnamon. Enjoy as a main course or appetizer at festive occasions and gatherings.

Recipe 35: Thai Red Curry Chicken

Preparation Time: 15 minutes
Cooking Time: 20 minutes
Total Time: 35 minutes
Servings: 4

Ingredients:
- 1 lb boneless, skinless chicken breast or thighs, cut into bite-sized pieces
- Salt and pepper to taste
- 2 tablespoons red curry paste
- 1 can (13.5 oz) coconut milk
- 1 red bell pepper, sliced
- 1 green bell pepper, sliced
- 1 onion, sliced
- 1 cup sliced mushrooms
- 1 tablespoon fish sauce
- 1 tablespoon brown sugar

- 1 tablespoon lime juice
- Fresh basil leaves for garnish
- Cooked rice for serving

Instructions:
1. Season the chicken pieces with salt and pepper on both sides.
2. Heat a large skillet or wok over medium heat. Add red curry paste and cook for 1-2 minutes, stirring constantly, until fragrant.
3. Pour in coconut milk and stir to combine with the curry paste. Bring to a simmer.
4. Add sliced chicken to the skillet or wok, stirring to coat with the curry sauce. Cook for 5 minutes.
5. Add sliced red bell pepper, green bell pepper, onion, and sliced mushrooms to the skillet or wok. Simmer for another 10 minutes, or until the vegetables are tender and the chicken is cooked through.
6. Stir in fish sauce, brown sugar, and lime juice. Taste and adjust seasoning if needed.
7. Remove from heat and garnish with fresh basil leaves.
8. Serve the Thai Red Curry Chicken hot over cooked rice.

Serving Suggestion: Thai Red Curry Chicken is traditionally served with steamed jasmine rice or Thai sticky rice. Garnish with additional fresh basil leaves and sliced red chili peppers for extra heat if desired. Enjoy with a side of Thai cucumber salad or stir-fried vegetables.

Recipe 36: Jamaican Curry Chicken

Preparation Time: 15 minutes
Cooking Time: 40 minutes
Total Time: 55 minutes
Servings: 4

Ingredients:
- 2 lbs chicken pieces (such as thighs and drumsticks), skin-on
- Salt and pepper to taste
- 2 tablespoons vegetable oil
- 1 onion, chopped
- 2 cloves garlic, minced
- 1 tablespoon Jamaican curry powder
- 1 teaspoon ground allspice
- 1 teaspoon dried thyme
- 1 teaspoon paprika
- 1/2 teaspoon cayenne pepper (adjust to taste)
- 1 cup chicken broth
- 2 potatoes, peeled and diced
- 1 carrot, diced
- 1 bell pepper, diced
- 1 tomato, diced
- 2 tablespoons chopped fresh cilantro

Instructions:
1. Season the chicken pieces with salt and pepper on both sides.
2. Heat vegetable oil in a large skillet or Dutch oven over medium-high heat. Add the chicken pieces and cook until browned on all sides. Remove from the skillet and set aside.
3. In the same skillet, add chopped onion and minced garlic. Cook until softened and fragrant.

4. Stir in Jamaican curry powder, ground allspice, dried thyme, paprika, and cayenne pepper. Cook for another minute until fragrant.
5. Return the browned chicken pieces to the skillet. Pour in chicken broth and bring to a simmer.
6. Cover the skillet and cook over low heat for 20-25 minutes, or until the chicken is cooked through and tender.
7. Add diced potatoes, diced carrot, diced bell pepper, and diced tomato to the skillet. Simmer for another 10-15 minutes, or until the vegetables are tender and the sauce has thickened.
8. Taste and adjust seasoning with salt and pepper if needed.
9. Remove from heat and garnish with chopped fresh cilantro.
10. Serve the Jamaican Curry Chicken hot, accompanied by rice and peas or Jamaican-style rice and beans.

Serving Suggestion: Jamaican Curry Chicken is traditionally served with rice and peas, boiled yams, and fried plantains. Enjoy with a glass of Jamaican ginger beer or coconut water for a taste of the Caribbean.

Recipe 37: Lebanese Chicken Fatteh

Preparation Time: 20 minutes
Cooking Time: 45 minutes
Total Time: 1 hour 5 minutes
Servings: 4

Ingredients:
- 2 lbs bone-in, skin-on chicken thighs
- Salt and pepper to taste
- 2 tablespoons olive oil
- 1 onion, finely chopped
- 4 cloves garlic, minced
- 1 teaspoon ground cumin
- 1 teaspoon ground coriander
- 1/2 teaspoon ground cinnamon
- 1/2 teaspoon paprika
- 1/4 teaspoon cayenne pepper
- 1 can (15 oz) chickpeas, drained and rinsed
- 2 cups chicken broth
- 4 cups stale pita bread, torn into bite-sized pieces
- 2 cups plain Greek yogurt
- 2 tablespoons tahini
- 2 tablespoons lemon juice
- 1/4 cup chopped fresh parsley
- 1/4 cup chopped fresh mint
- Pine nuts for garnish
- Sumac for garnish

Instructions:
1. Season the chicken thighs with salt and pepper on both sides.
2. Heat olive oil in a large skillet or Dutch oven over medium-high heat. Add the chicken thighs and cook until browned on both sides. Remove from the skillet and set aside.
3. In the same skillet, add finely chopped onion and minced garlic. Cook until softened and translucent.
4. Stir in ground cumin, ground coriander, ground cinnamon, paprika, and cayenne pepper. Cook for another minute until fragrant.

5. Return the browned chicken thighs to the skillet. Add chickpeas and chicken broth. Bring to a simmer.
6. Cover the skillet and cook over low heat for 30-35 minutes, or until the chicken is cooked through and tender.
7. Remove the chicken thighs from the skillet and shred the meat using two forks. Return the shredded chicken to the skillet and stir to combine with the chickpeas and sauce.
8. Preheat the oven to 350°F (175°C). Arrange the torn pita bread pieces on a baking sheet and bake in the preheated oven for 10-15 minutes, or until crispy and golden brown.
9. In a bowl, whisk together plain Greek yogurt, tahini, and lemon juice until smooth.
10. To assemble the Fatteh, spread the baked pita bread pieces on the bottom of a serving platter or individual serving bowls.
11. Spoon the chicken and chickpea mixture over the pita bread.
12. Drizzle the yogurt-tahini sauce over the top.
13. Garnish with chopped fresh parsley, chopped fresh mint, pine nuts, and a sprinkle of sumac.
14. Serve the Lebanese Chicken Fatteh warm.

Serving Suggestion: Lebanese Chicken Fatteh is traditionally served as a main dish or part of a mezze spread. Enjoy with additional yogurt-tahini sauce on the side and a fresh salad of chopped tomatoes, cucumbers, and lettuce.

Recipe 38: Turkish Chicken Pilaf (Tavuk Pilavı)

Preparation Time: 15 minutes
Cooking Time: 30 minutes
Total Time: 45 minutes
Servings: 4

Ingredients:
- 1 lb boneless, skinless chicken breast or thighs, cut into bite-sized pieces
- Salt and pepper to taste
- 2 tablespoons olive oil
- 1 onion, chopped
- 2 cloves garlic, minced
- 1 cup long-grain white rice
- 2 cups chicken broth
- 1/2 cup frozen peas
- 1/4 cup chopped fresh parsley
- Lemon wedges for serving

Instructions:
1. Season the chicken pieces with salt and pepper on both sides.
2. Heat olive oil in a large skillet or Dutch oven over medium-high heat. Add the chicken pieces and cook until browned on all sides. Remove from the skillet and set aside.
3. In the same skillet, add chopped onion and minced garlic. Cook until softened and translucent.
4. Stir in long-grain white rice and cook for another 2-3 minutes, stirring frequently, until lightly toasted.
5. Return the browned chicken pieces to the skillet. Pour in chicken broth and bring to a simmer.
6. Cover the skillet and cook over low heat for 15-20 minutes, or until the rice is tender and has absorbed the liquid.

7. Stir in frozen peas and chopped fresh parsley. Cook for another 2-3 minutes, until the peas are heated through.
8. Taste and adjust seasoning with salt and pepper if needed.
9. Serve the Turkish Chicken Pilaf hot, accompanied by lemon wedges for squeezing over the rice.

Serving Suggestion: Turkish Chicken Pilaf is traditionally served as a main dish or part of a larger meal. Enjoy with a side of Turkish salad, pickled vegetables, or yogurt cucumber dip. Pair with Turkish ayran (yogurt drink) or Turkish tea for a complete Turkish dining experience.

Recipe 39: Vietnamese Lemongrass Chicken

Preparation Time: 20 minutes (plus marinating time)
Cooking Time: 15 minutes
Total Time: 35 minutes (plus marinating time)
Servings: 4

Ingredients:
- 1 lb boneless, skinless chicken thighs, thinly sliced
- Salt and pepper to taste
- 2 stalks lemongrass, white parts only, finely minced
- 4 cloves garlic, minced
- 2 shallots, minced
- 2 tablespoons fish sauce
- 1 tablespoon soy sauce
- 1 tablespoon honey
- 1 tablespoon vegetable oil

- 1 tablespoon sesame oil
- 1 tablespoon lime juice
- 1 teaspoon chili flakes (optional)
- Fresh cilantro for garnish
- Cooked rice or vermicelli noodles for serving
- Lime wedges for serving

Instructions:
1. In a bowl, combine minced lemongrass, minced garlic, minced shallots, fish sauce, soy sauce, honey, vegetable oil, sesame oil, lime juice, salt, pepper, and chili flakes (if using). Mix well to make the marinade.
2. Add the thinly sliced chicken thighs to the marinade, tossing to coat evenly. Cover and refrigerate for at least 1 hour, or overnight for best flavor.
3. Heat a skillet or grill pan over medium-high heat. Remove the chicken from the marinade and discard any excess marinade.
4. Cook the marinated chicken slices in batches for 3-4 minutes on each side, or until browned and cooked through.
5. Remove from the skillet and transfer to a serving platter.
6. Garnish the Vietnamese Lemongrass Chicken with fresh cilantro and serve hot with cooked rice or vermicelli noodles.
7. Serve with lime wedges on the side for squeezing over the chicken.

Serving Suggestion: Vietnamese Lemongrass Chicken is traditionally served with steamed jasmine rice or vermicelli noodles. Enjoy with a side of pickled vegetables and Vietnamese dipping sauce (nuoc cham) for a complete Vietnamese meal experience.

Recipe 40: Argentinean Chicken Milanesa

Preparation Time: 20 minutes
Cooking Time: 15 minutes
Total Time: 35 minutes
Servings: 4

Ingredients:
- 4 boneless, skinless chicken breasts
- Salt and pepper to taste
- 1 cup all-purpose flour
- 2 eggs, beaten
- 1 cup breadcrumbs
- Vegetable oil for frying
- Lemon wedges for serving
- Fresh parsley for garnish
- Cooked French fries or mashed potatoes for serving

Instructions:
1. Place each chicken breast between two sheets of plastic wrap. Pound with a meat mallet or rolling pin until about 1/4 inch thick. Season both sides with salt and pepper.
2. Set up a breading station with three shallow dishes: one with all-purpose flour, one with beaten eggs, and one with breadcrumbs.
3. Dredge each chicken breast in flour, shaking off any excess. Dip into beaten eggs, then coat evenly with breadcrumbs, pressing gently to adhere.

4. Heat vegetable oil in a large skillet or deep fryer to 350°F (175°C).
5. Carefully add the breaded chicken breasts to the hot oil and fry for 3-4 minutes on each side, or until golden brown and cooked through.
6. Remove from the oil and drain on paper towels.
7. Serve the Argentinean Chicken Milanesa hot, garnished with fresh parsley and lemon wedges on the side.
8. Serve with cooked French fries or mashed potatoes as a classic side dish.

Serving Suggestion: Argentinean Chicken Milanesa is traditionally served with lemon wedges for squeezing over the crispy chicken. Enjoy with a side of mixed greens or a simple salad dressed with vinaigrette.

Recipe 41: Filipino Chicken Tinola

Preparation Time: 15 minutes
Cooking Time: 30 minutes
Total Time: 45 minutes
Servings: 4

Ingredients:
- 1 lb chicken pieces (such as thighs and drumsticks), skin-on
- Salt and pepper to taste
- 2 tablespoons vegetable oil
- 1 onion, sliced
- 3 cloves garlic, minced
- 1 thumb-sized piece of ginger, sliced
- 2 cups water

- 1 medium-sized green papaya, peeled, seeded, and sliced
- 2 cups spinach leaves
- 1 tablespoon fish sauce (patis)
- Fresh cilantro or green onions for garnish
- Cooked rice for serving

Instructions:
1. Season the chicken pieces with salt and pepper on both sides.
2. Heat vegetable oil in a large pot over medium heat. Add sliced onion, minced garlic, and sliced ginger. Cook until softened and fragrant.
3. Add the seasoned chicken pieces to the pot. Brown on all sides for about 5 minutes.
4. Pour in water and bring to a simmer. Cover and cook over medium-low heat for 15 minutes.
5. Add sliced green papaya to the pot and continue simmering for another 10 minutes, or until the chicken is cooked through and the papaya is tender.
6. Stir in fish sauce and adjust seasoning with salt and pepper if needed.
7. Add spinach leaves to the pot and cook for an additional 2-3 minutes, until wilted.
8. Remove from heat and garnish the Filipino Chicken Tinola with fresh cilantro or green onions.
9. Serve hot with cooked rice.

Serving Suggestion: Filipino Chicken Tinola is traditionally served as a hearty soup dish, accompanied by cooked rice. Enjoy with a side of fish sauce (patis) with calamansi or lemon juice for dipping the chicken and vegetables.

Recipe 42: Ethiopian Doro Tibs

Preparation Time: 20 minutes
Cooking Time: 40 minutes
Total Time: 1 hour
Servings: 4

Ingredients:
- 1 lb boneless, skinless chicken breast or thighs, cut into bite-sized pieces
- Salt and pepper to taste
- 2 tablespoons clarified butter (niter kibbeh) or vegetable oil
- 1 onion, finely chopped
- 3 cloves garlic, minced
- 1 tablespoon grated fresh ginger
- 2 tomatoes, chopped
- 1 tablespoon berbere spice blend
- 1/2 teaspoon ground turmeric
- 1/2 teaspoon ground cumin
- 1/2 teaspoon ground coriander
- 1/4 teaspoon ground cardamom
- 1/4 teaspoon ground fenugreek
- 1/4 cup water or chicken broth
- Fresh cilantro for garnish
- Injera or cooked rice for serving

Instructions:
1. Season the chicken pieces with salt and pepper on both sides.
2. Heat clarified butter or vegetable oil in a large skillet or Dutch oven over medium heat.

3. Add finely chopped onion, minced garlic, and grated fresh ginger to the skillet. Cook until softened and fragrant.
4. Stir in chopped tomatoes and cook until softened, breaking them down with the back of a spoon.
5. Add berbere spice blend, ground turmeric, ground cumin, ground coriander, ground cardamom, and ground fenugreek to the skillet. Cook for another minute until fragrant.
6. Add the seasoned chicken pieces to the skillet and stir to coat with the spice mixture.
7. Pour in water or chicken broth and bring to a simmer. Cover and cook over low heat for 20-25 minutes, or until the chicken is cooked through and tender.
8. Taste and adjust seasoning with salt and pepper if needed.
9. Garnish the Ethiopian Doro Tibs with fresh cilantro.
10. Serve hot with injera or cooked rice.

Serving Suggestion: Ethiopian Doro Tibs is traditionally served as a main dish, accompanied by injera (Ethiopian flatbread) or cooked rice. Enjoy with additional injera for scooping up the flavorful chicken and sauce.

Recipe 43: Russian Chicken Kotleti

Preparation Time: 20 minutes
Cooking Time: 20 minutes
Total Time: 40 minutes
Servings: 4

Ingredients:
- 1 lb ground chicken
- 1 onion, grated
- 2 cloves garlic, minced
- 1/4 cup breadcrumbs
- 1 egg
- 2 tablespoons chopped fresh dill
- 2 tablespoons chopped fresh parsley
- Salt and pepper to taste
- Vegetable oil for frying
- Sour cream for serving
- Mashed potatoes or buckwheat kasha for serving

Instructions:
1. In a large bowl, combine ground chicken, grated onion, minced garlic, breadcrumbs, egg, chopped fresh dill, chopped fresh parsley, salt, and pepper. Mix well to combine.
2. Shape the chicken mixture into oval-shaped patties, about 1/2 inch thick.
3. Heat vegetable oil in a large skillet over medium heat.
4. Working in batches, carefully add the chicken kotleti to the hot oil and fry for 4-5 minutes on each side, or until golden brown and cooked through.
5. Remove from the oil and drain on paper towels.
6. Serve the Russian Chicken Kotleti hot, accompanied by sour cream for dipping.
7. Serve with mashed potatoes or buckwheat kasha as a classic side dish.

Serving Suggestion: Russian Chicken Kotleti are traditionally served as a main dish, accompanied by sour cream for dipping. Enjoy with a side of mashed potatoes or buckwheat kasha for a comforting and satisfying meal.

Recipe 44: Thai Chicken Larb

Preparation Time: 15 minutes
Cooking Time: 15 minutes
Total Time: 30 minutes
Servings: 4

Ingredients:
- 1 lb ground chicken
- 2 tablespoons vegetable oil
- 2 shallots, thinly sliced
- 3 cloves garlic, minced
- 1 tablespoon grated fresh ginger
- 2 tablespoons fish sauce
- 2 tablespoons lime juice
- 1 tablespoon soy sauce
- 1 tablespoon brown sugar
- 1 teaspoon chili flakes (adjust to taste)
- 1/4 cup chopped fresh cilantro
- 1/4 cup chopped fresh mint
- 1/4 cup chopped fresh basil
- Lettuce leaves for serving
- Cooked rice or sticky rice for serving

Instructions:
1. Heat vegetable oil in a large skillet or wok over medium-high heat.
2. Add thinly sliced shallots to the skillet and cook until softened and lightly caramelized.
3. Stir in minced garlic and grated fresh ginger. Cook for another minute until fragrant.

4. Add ground chicken to the skillet and cook, breaking it up with a spoon, until browned and cooked through.
5. In a small bowl, whisk together fish sauce, lime juice, soy sauce, brown sugar, and chili flakes.
6. Pour the sauce mixture over the cooked chicken in the skillet. Stir to combine and cook for another 2-3 minutes.
7. Remove from heat and stir in chopped fresh cilantro, chopped fresh mint, and chopped fresh basil.
8. Taste and adjust seasoning with additional fish sauce, lime juice, or chili flakes if needed.
9. Serve the Thai Chicken Larb hot, spooned into lettuce leaves.
10. Serve with cooked rice or sticky rice on the side.

Serving Suggestion: Thai Chicken Larb is traditionally served as a main dish or appetizer, wrapped in lettuce leaves. Enjoy with cooked rice or sticky rice for a complete and satisfying meal.

Recipe 45: Cuban Chicken Fricassee

Preparation Time: 20 minutes
Cooking Time: 40 minutes
Total Time: 1 hour
Servings: 4

Ingredients:
- 1 whole chicken, cut into serving pieces
- Salt and pepper to taste
- 2 tablespoons olive oil

- 1 onion, chopped
- 1 bell pepper, chopped
- 3 cloves garlic, minced
- 1 tomato, chopped
- 1 cup chicken broth
- 1/4 cup dry white wine
- 1/4 cup pimento-stuffed green olives
- 2 tablespoons capers
- 1 tablespoon tomato paste
- 1 teaspoon ground cumin
- 1 teaspoon dried oregano
- 1 bay leaf
- 1/4 cup chopped fresh cilantro
- Cooked rice for serving
- Lime wedges for serving

Instructions:
1. Season the chicken pieces with salt and pepper on both sides.
2. Heat olive oil in a large skillet or Dutch oven over medium-high heat. Add the chicken pieces and cook until browned on all sides. Remove from the skillet and set aside.
3. In the same skillet, add chopped onion and chopped bell pepper. Cook until softened.
4. Stir in minced garlic and cook for another minute until fragrant.
5. Add chopped tomato, chicken broth, dry white wine, pimento-stuffed green olives, capers, tomato paste, ground cumin, dried oregano, and bay leaf to the skillet. Stir to combine.
6. Return the browned chicken pieces to the skillet, along with any accumulated juices. Bring to a simmer.

7. Cover the skillet and cook over low heat for 30-35 minutes, or until the chicken is cooked through and tender.
8. Remove the bay leaf from the skillet and discard.
9. Taste and adjust seasoning with salt and pepper if needed.
10. Garnish the Cuban Chicken Fricassee with chopped fresh cilantro.
11. Serve hot with cooked rice and lime wedges on the side.

Serving Suggestion: Cuban Chicken Fricassee is traditionally served as a main dish, accompanied by cooked rice. Squeeze fresh lime juice over the chicken before enjoying for a burst of citrus flavor.

Recipe 46: Pakistani Chicken Karahi

Preparation Time: 15 minutes
Cooking Time: 30 minutes
Total Time: 45 minutes
Servings: 4

Ingredients:
- 1 lb chicken, cut into bite-sized pieces
- Salt to taste
- 1/4 cup vegetable oil
- 2 onions, finely sliced
- 3 tomatoes, chopped
- 2 green chilies, sliced
- 1 tablespoon ginger paste
- 1 tablespoon garlic paste

- 1 teaspoon cumin seeds
- 1 teaspoon coriander powder
- 1/2 teaspoon red chili powder
- 1/2 teaspoon turmeric powder
- 1/2 teaspoon garam masala
- Fresh cilantro leaves for garnish

Instructions:
1. Season the chicken pieces with salt and set aside.
2. Heat vegetable oil in a karahi or large skillet over medium heat.
3. Add cumin seeds and let them sizzle for a few seconds.
4. Add finely sliced onions and cook until they turn golden brown.
5. Stir in ginger paste and garlic paste, and cook for another minute.
6. Add chopped tomatoes and green chilies, and cook until the tomatoes are softened and the oil starts to separate.
7. Add coriander powder, red chili powder, turmeric powder, and garam masala. Cook for a minute.
8. Add the seasoned chicken pieces to the skillet and mix well with the masala.
9. Cover and cook for 20-25 minutes, stirring occasionally, until the chicken is cooked through and the sauce thickens.
10. Garnish the Pakistani Chicken Karahi with fresh cilantro leaves.
11. Serve hot with naan or rice.

Serving Suggestion: Pakistani Chicken Karahi is traditionally served with naan or rice. Enjoy with a side of raita (yogurt sauce) and salad for a complete meal.

Recipe 47: Malaysian Chicken Rendang

Preparation Time: 20 minutes
Cooking Time: 1 hour 30 minutes
Total Time: 1 hour 50 minutes
Servings: 4

Ingredients:
- 2 lbs chicken thighs, bone-in and skinless, cut into pieces
- Salt to taste
- 2 tablespoons vegetable oil
- 1 onion, chopped
- 3 cloves garlic, minced
- 1 thumb-sized piece of ginger, grated
- 2 stalks lemongrass, bruised
- 4 kaffir lime leaves
- 1 cinnamon stick
- 4 cardamom pods
- 1 star anise
- 1 cup coconut milk
- 1 cup water
- 1 tablespoon tamarind paste
- 2 tablespoons grated palm sugar or brown sugar
- Salt to taste

Spice Paste (Rendang Paste):
- 6 dried red chilies, soaked in hot water and deseeded
- 4 shallots, chopped
- 3 cloves garlic, chopped
- 1 thumb-sized piece of ginger, chopped

- 1 thumb-sized piece of galangal, chopped
- 1 tablespoon coriander seeds
- 1 teaspoon cumin seeds
- 1 teaspoon fennel seeds
- 1/2 teaspoon ground turmeric

Instructions:
1. Season the chicken pieces with salt and set aside.
2. Heat vegetable oil in a large pot over medium heat. Add the spice paste ingredients and cook until fragrant.
3. Add chopped onions, minced garlic, and grated ginger. Cook until the onions are soft and translucent.
4. Add lemongrass, kaffir lime leaves, cinnamon stick, cardamom pods, and star anise. Stir well.
5. Add the chicken pieces to the pot and stir to coat with the spice mixture.
6. Pour in coconut milk and water. Bring to a boil.
7. Reduce the heat to low and simmer uncovered for about 1 hour, stirring occasionally, until the sauce thickens and the chicken is tender.
8. Stir in tamarind paste and grated palm sugar. Cook for another 10-15 minutes.
9. Adjust salt to taste.
10. Remove from heat and serve the Malaysian Chicken Rendang hot with steamed rice.

Serving Suggestion: Malaysian Chicken Rendang is traditionally served with steamed rice. Enjoy with a side of cucumber slices and sambal belacan (spicy shrimp paste) for an authentic Malaysian meal experience.

Recipe 48: Italian Chicken Marsala

Preparation Time: 10 minutes
Cooking Time: 20 minutes
Total Time: 30 minutes
Servings: 4

Ingredients:
- 4 boneless, skinless chicken breasts
- Salt and pepper to taste
- 1/2 cup all-purpose flour
- 4 tablespoons unsalted butter
- 4 tablespoons olive oil
- 8 ounces mushrooms, sliced
- 2 cloves garlic, minced
- 1 cup Marsala wine
- 1 cup chicken broth
- 2 tablespoons chopped fresh parsley

Instructions:
1. Place each chicken breast between two sheets of plastic wrap. Pound with a meat mallet or rolling pin until about 1/4 inch thick. Season both sides with salt and pepper.
2. Dredge the chicken breasts in flour, shaking off any excess.
3. In a large skillet, heat 2 tablespoons of butter and 2 tablespoons of olive oil over medium-high heat.
4. Add the chicken breasts to the skillet and cook for 3-4 minutes on each side, or until golden brown and cooked through. Remove from the skillet and set aside.

5. In the same skillet, add the remaining butter and olive oil. Add the sliced mushrooms and minced garlic. Cook until the mushrooms are golden brown and the liquid has evaporated.
6. Pour in the Marsala wine and chicken broth. Bring to a simmer and cook for 5-7 minutes, or until the sauce is slightly reduced.
7. Return the cooked chicken breasts to the skillet. Simmer for another 2-3 minutes to heat through and coat the chicken with the sauce.
8. Garnish the Italian Chicken Marsala with chopped fresh parsley.
9. Serve hot with pasta or mashed potatoes.

Serving Suggestion: Italian Chicken Marsala is traditionally served with pasta or mashed potatoes. Enjoy with a side of steamed vegetables or a green salad for a delicious Italian meal.

Recipe 49: Greek Chicken Gyro

Preparation Time: 15 minutes
Marinating Time: 1 hour (optional)
Cooking Time: 15 minutes
Total Time: 1 hour 30 minutes (if marinating)
Servings: 4

Ingredients:
- 1 lb chicken breast or thigh, thinly sliced
- Salt and pepper to taste
- 4 pita bread
- Tzatziki sauce (store-bought or homemade) for serving

- Sliced tomatoes for serving
- Sliced cucumbers for serving
- Sliced red onions for serving
- Fresh lettuce leaves for serving
- Lemon wedges for serving

Marinade:
- 1/4 cup Greek yogurt
- 2 tablespoons olive oil
- 2 cloves garlic, minced
- 1 tablespoon lemon juice
- 1 teaspoon dried oregano
- 1 teaspoon dried thyme
- 1 teaspoon paprika
- 1/2 teaspoon ground cumin
- 1/2 teaspoon ground coriander
- 1/2 teaspoon salt
- 1/4 teaspoon black pepper

Instructions:
1. In a bowl, combine all the marinade ingredients.
Add the thinly sliced chicken and toss to coat evenly.
Cover and refrigerate for at least 1 hour, or overnight
for best flavor (optional).
2. Heat a grill pan or skillet over medium-high heat.
Cook the marinated chicken slices for 3-4 minutes on
each side, or until cooked through and lightly charred.
3. Warm the pita bread in the oven or on the grill for a
few minutes.
4. Spread tzatziki sauce on each pita bread.
5. Arrange the cooked chicken slices, sliced tomatoes,
sliced cucumbers, sliced red onions, and lettuce leaves
on top of the tzatziki sauce.
6. Squeeze fresh lemon juice over the gyro filling.
7. Roll up the pita bread tightly, enclosing the filling.

8. Serve the Greek Chicken Gyro immediately.

Serving Suggestion: Greek Chicken Gyro is traditionally served as a handheld street food. Enjoy with additional tzatziki sauce and lemon wedges on the side. Serve with Greek salad or fries for a complete meal.

Recipe 50: Japanese Chicken Yakitori

Preparation Time: 15 minutes
Marinating Time: 30 minutes
Cooking Time: 10 minutes
Total Time: 55 minutes
Servings: 4

Ingredients:
- 1 lb boneless, skinless chicken thighs, cut into bite-sized pieces
- Bamboo skewers, soaked in water for 30 minutes
- Salt and pepper to taste
- 2 tablespoons soy sauce
- 2 tablespoons mirin
- 1 tablespoon sake (Japanese rice wine)
- 1 tablespoon honey
- 1 clove garlic, minced
- 1 teaspoon grated ginger

- Thinly sliced green onions for garnish
- Toasted sesame seeds for garnish

Instructions:
1. Season the chicken thigh pieces with salt and pepper.
2. In a bowl, whisk together soy sauce, mirin, sake, honey, minced garlic, and grated ginger to make the marinade.
3. Add the chicken pieces to the marinade and toss to coat evenly. Cover and refrigerate for at least 30 minutes.
4. Thread the marinated chicken pieces onto the soaked bamboo skewers.
5. Preheat a grill or grill pan over medium-high heat.
6. Grill the chicken skewers for 3-4 minutes on each side, or until cooked through and lightly charred.
7. Transfer the grilled chicken yakitori skewers to a serving platter.
8. Garnish with thinly sliced green onions and toasted sesame seeds.
9. Serve hot as an appetizer or with steamed rice as a main dish.

Serving Suggestion: Japanese Chicken Yakitori is traditionally served as a popular street food or izakaya (Japanese pub) snack. Enjoy with a side of pickled vegetables and a cold beer or sake for a delightful Japanese dining experience.

Recipe 51: Indian Chicken Tikka Masala

Preparation Time: 20 minutes (plus marinating time)
Cooking Time: 30 minutes
Total Time: 50 minutes (plus marinating time)
Servings: 4

Ingredients:
- 1 lb boneless, skinless chicken thighs or breast, cut into bite-sized pieces
- Salt to taste
- 1 cup plain yogurt
- 2 tablespoons vegetable oil
- 1 onion, finely chopped
- 3 cloves garlic, minced
- 1 tablespoon grated fresh ginger
- 1 cup tomato puree
- 1 tablespoon tomato paste
- 1 tablespoon ground coriander
- 1 tablespoon ground cumin
- 1 teaspoon ground turmeric
- 1 teaspoon paprika
- 1/2 teaspoon cayenne pepper (adjust to taste)
- 1/2 cup heavy cream
- Fresh cilantro leaves for garnish

Instructions:
1. Season the chicken pieces with salt and set aside.
2. In a bowl, combine plain yogurt with ground coriander, ground cumin, ground turmeric, paprika, and cayenne pepper. Add the chicken pieces to the marinade, toss to coat evenly, cover, and refrigerate for at least 1 hour, or overnight for best flavor.
3. Heat vegetable oil in a large skillet or Dutch oven over medium-high heat.

4. Add finely chopped onion and cook until softened and translucent.
5. Stir in minced garlic and grated fresh ginger. Cook for another minute until fragrant.
6. Add tomato puree and tomato paste to the skillet. Cook until the oil starts to separate from the sauce.
7. Add the marinated chicken pieces to the skillet along with any remaining marinade. Cook for 8-10 minutes, stirring occasionally, until the chicken is cooked through.
8. Stir in heavy cream and simmer for another 5 minutes, stirring occasionally, until the sauce thickens.
9. Adjust seasoning with salt if needed.
10. Garnish the Indian Chicken Tikka Masala with fresh cilantro leaves.
11. Serve hot with steamed rice or naan.

Serving Suggestion: Indian Chicken Tikka Masala is traditionally served with basmati rice or naan bread. Enjoy with a side of cucumber raita (yogurt sauce) and mango chutney for a burst of flavor.

Recipe 52: Spanish Chicken Paella Valenciana

Preparation Time: 20 minutes
Cooking Time: 40 minutes
Total Time: 1 hour
Servings: 4

Ingredients:
- 1 lb chicken thighs, bone-in and skin-on, cut into pieces
- Salt and pepper to taste

- 2 tablespoons olive oil
- 1 onion, diced
- 2 cloves garlic, minced
- 1 red bell pepper, sliced
- 1 green bell pepper, sliced
- 1 tomato, diced
- 1 cup Arborio rice
- 2 cups chicken broth
- 1/2 teaspoon saffron threads
- 1/2 teaspoon smoked paprika
- 1/2 cup frozen peas
- 1/4 cup chopped fresh parsley
- Lemon wedges for serving

Instructions:
1. Season the chicken pieces with salt and pepper.
2. Heat olive oil in a paella pan or large skillet over medium-high heat.
3. Add the chicken pieces to the pan and cook until browned on all sides. Remove from the pan and set aside.
4. In the same pan, add diced onion and minced garlic. Cook until softened and fragrant.
5. Add sliced red and green bell peppers to the pan. Cook until they start to soften.
6. Stir in diced tomato and cook until it breaks down and releases its juices.
7. Add Arborio rice to the pan and stir to coat in the vegetable mixture.
8. Pour in chicken broth and add saffron threads and smoked paprika. Stir to combine.
9. Arrange the browned chicken pieces on top of the rice mixture.
10. Cover the pan and simmer for about 20 minutes, or until the rice is cooked and the chicken is tender.

11. Sprinkle frozen peas over the paella and cook for another 5 minutes, or until heated through.
12. Garnish with chopped fresh parsley and serve hot with lemon wedges on the side.

Serving Suggestion: Spanish Chicken Paella Valenciana is traditionally served as a main dish. Enjoy with a side of crusty bread and a glass of Spanish wine for an authentic dining experience.

Recipe 53: Korean Spicy Chicken Stew (Dakdoritang)

Preparation Time: 20 minutes
Cooking Time: 40 minutes
Total Time: 1 hour
Servings: 4

Ingredients:
- 2 lbs chicken pieces (legs, thighs, or wings), skin-on
- Salt and pepper to taste
- 2 tablespoons vegetable oil
- 1 onion, sliced
- 4 cloves garlic, minced
- 1 thumb-sized piece of ginger, sliced
- 2 potatoes, peeled and cut into chunks
- 2 carrots, peeled and cut into chunks
- 1/2 cup Korean red chili paste (gochujang)
- 1/4 cup Korean red chili flakes (gochugaru)
- 2 tablespoons soy sauce

- 1 tablespoon sugar
- 4 cups chicken broth
- 2 green onions, chopped
- Cooked rice for serving

Instructions:
1. Season the chicken pieces with salt and pepper.
2. Heat vegetable oil in a large pot or Dutch oven over medium-high heat.
3. Add the chicken pieces to the pot and brown on all sides. Remove from the pot and set aside.
4. In the same pot, add sliced onion, minced garlic, and sliced ginger. Cook until softened and fragrant.
5. Stir in chunks of potatoes and carrots, and cook for a few minutes.
6. Add Korean red chili paste (gochujang), Korean red chili flakes (gochugaru), soy sauce, and sugar to the pot. Stir to coat the vegetables.
7. Return the browned chicken pieces to the pot and pour in chicken broth.
8. Bring to a boil, then reduce the heat to low and simmer, covered, for about 30 minutes, or until the chicken is cooked through and the vegetables are tender.
9. Adjust seasoning with salt and pepper if needed.
10. Garnish the Korean Spicy Chicken Stew with chopped green onions.
11. Serve hot with cooked rice.

Serving Suggestion: Korean Spicy Chicken Stew (Dakdoritang) is traditionally served as a main dish. Enjoy with a side of kimchi and steamed rice for a comforting and spicy meal.

Recipe 54: Brazilian Chicken Stroganoff

Preparation Time: 15 minutes
Cooking Time: 30 minutes
Total Time: 45 minutes
Servings: 4

Ingredients:
- 1 lb chicken breast, cut into strips
- Salt and pepper to taste
- 2 tablespoons butter
- 1 onion, finely chopped
- 2 cloves garlic, minced
- 1 red bell pepper, sliced
- 1 green bell pepper, sliced
- 1 cup sliced mushrooms
- 1 cup chicken broth
- 1 cup heavy cream
- 2 tablespoons tomato paste
- 2 tablespoons ketchup
- 1 tablespoon Worcestershire sauce
- 1 tablespoon mustard
- Cooked white rice for serving
- Chopped fresh parsley for garnish

Instructions:
1. Season the chicken strips with salt and pepper.
2. Heat butter in a large skillet over medium-high heat.
3. Add the chicken strips to the skillet and cook until browned on all sides. Remove from the skillet and set aside.

4. In the same skillet, add finely chopped onion and minced garlic. Cook until softened and fragrant.
5. Add sliced red and green bell peppers, and sliced mushrooms to the skillet. Cook until they start to soften.
6. Return the browned chicken strips to the skillet.
7. In a bowl, mix together chicken broth, heavy cream, tomato paste, ketchup, Worcestershire sauce, and mustard. Pour the mixture over the chicken and vegetables in the skillet.
8. Bring to a simmer and cook for about 10 minutes, or until the sauce thickens and the chicken is cooked through.
9. Adjust seasoning with salt and pepper if needed.
10. Serve the Brazilian Chicken Stroganoff hot over cooked white rice.
11. Garnish with chopped fresh parsley.

Serving Suggestion: Brazilian Chicken Stroganoff is traditionally served with white rice. Enjoy with a side of Brazilian-style black beans and farofa (toasted cassava flour) for a complete meal.

Recipe 55: Mexican Chicken Tinga

Preparation Time: 15 minutes
Cooking Time: 30 minutes
Total Time: 45 minutes
Servings: 4

Ingredients:
- 1 lb boneless, skinless chicken breasts
- Salt and pepper to taste

- 2 tablespoons vegetable oil
- 1 onion, thinly sliced
- 2 cloves garlic, minced
- 2 tomatoes, chopped
- 2 chipotle peppers in adobo sauce, chopped
- 1 teaspoon dried oregano
- 1 teaspoon ground cumin
- 1/2 cup chicken broth
- 2 tablespoons tomato paste
- 1 tablespoon lime juice
- Corn tortillas for serving
- Chopped fresh cilantro for garnish
- Sliced avocado for serving

Instructions:
1. Season the chicken breasts with salt and pepper.
2. Heat vegetable oil in a large skillet over medium-high heat.
3. Add the chicken breasts to the skillet and cook for 5-6 minutes on each side, or until cooked through. Remove from the skillet and shred the chicken using two forks. Set aside.
4. In the same skillet, add thinly sliced onion and minced garlic. Cook until softened and fragrant.
5. Add chopped tomatoes, chipotle peppers in adobo sauce, dried oregano, and ground cumin to the skillet. Cook until the tomatoes break down and release their juices.
6. Return the shredded chicken to the skillet.
7. Stir in chicken broth, tomato paste, and lime juice. Bring to a simmer and cook for another 10-15 minutes, or until the sauce thickens and flavors meld together.
8. Adjust seasoning with salt and pepper if needed.

9. Serve the Mexican Chicken Tinga hot with warm corn tortillas.
10. Garnish with chopped fresh cilantro and sliced avocado.

Serving Suggestion: Mexican Chicken Tinga is traditionally served as a filling for tacos or tostadas. Enjoy with a side of Mexican rice and refried beans for a delicious and satisfying meal.

Recipe 56: Moroccan Chicken Couscous

Preparation Time: 20 minutes
Cooking Time: 40 minutes
Total Time: 1 hour
Servings: 4

Ingredients:
- 1 lb chicken thighs, bone-in and skin-on
- Salt and pepper to taste
- 2 tablespoons olive oil
- 1 onion, finely chopped
- 2 cloves garlic, minced
- 1 teaspoon ground cumin
- 1 teaspoon ground coriander
- 1/2 teaspoon ground cinnamon
- 1/2 teaspoon ground ginger
- 1/4 teaspoon ground turmeric
- 1/4 teaspoon cayenne pepper

- 1 cup chicken broth
- 1 can (15 ounces) chickpeas, drained and rinsed
- 1 cup diced carrots
- 1 cup diced zucchini
- 1 cup diced bell peppers (any color)
- 1 cup diced tomatoes
- 1 cup chicken broth
- 1 cup couscous
- Chopped fresh parsley for garnish
- Lemon wedges for serving

Instructions:
1. Season the chicken thighs with salt and pepper.
2. Heat olive oil in a large pot or Dutch oven over medium-high heat.
3. Add the chicken thighs to the pot and cook until browned on all sides. Remove from the pot and set aside.
4. In the same pot, add finely chopped onion and minced garlic. Cook until softened and fragrant.
5. Add ground cumin, ground coriander, ground cinnamon, ground ginger, ground turmeric, and cayenne pepper to the pot. Cook for another minute until fragrant.
6. Return the browned chicken thighs to the pot.
7. Pour in chicken broth and bring to a simmer. Cover and cook for 20 minutes.
8. Add drained and rinsed chickpeas, diced carrots, diced zucchini, diced bell peppers, and diced tomatoes to the pot. Stir to combine.
9. Cover and cook for another 15-20 minutes, or until the chicken is cooked through and the vegetables are tender.

10. In a separate saucepan, bring chicken broth to a boil. Stir in couscous, cover, and remove from heat. Let stand for 5 minutes, then fluff with a fork.
11. Serve the Moroccan Chicken Couscous hot, spooned over the cooked couscous.
12. Garnish with chopped fresh parsley and serve with lemon wedges on the side.

Serving Suggestion: Moroccan Chicken Couscous is traditionally served as a main dish. Enjoy with a side of Moroccan-style flatbread and mint tea for an authentic Moroccan dining experience.

Recipe 57: Thai Pineapple Chicken Curry

Preparation Time: 15 minutes
Cooking Time: 30 minutes
Total Time: 45 minutes
Servings: 4

Ingredients:
- 1 lb boneless, skinless chicken thighs, cut into bite-sized pieces
- Salt and pepper to taste
- 2 tablespoons red curry paste
- 1 can (14 ounces) coconut milk
- 1 cup chicken broth
- 2 tablespoons fish sauce
- 1 tablespoon palm sugar or brown sugar
- 1 cup diced pineapple (fresh or canned)
- 1 red bell pepper, sliced
- 1 green bell pepper, sliced
- Fresh Thai basil leaves for garnish

- Cooked jasmine rice for serving

Instructions:
1. Season the chicken thigh pieces with salt and pepper.
2. In a large skillet or wok, heat red curry paste over medium heat for 1-2 minutes until fragrant.
3. Add chicken pieces to the skillet and cook until browned on all sides.
4. Pour in coconut milk, chicken broth, fish sauce, and palm sugar. Stir to combine.
5. Bring the mixture to a simmer and cook for about 15 minutes, stirring occasionally.
6. Add diced pineapple, sliced red bell pepper, and sliced green bell pepper to the skillet. Stir to combine.
7. Continue to simmer for another 10-15 minutes, or until the chicken is cooked through and the vegetables are tender.
8. Adjust seasoning with salt, pepper, or more fish sauce if needed.
9. Garnish the Thai Pineapple Chicken Curry with fresh Thai basil leaves.
10. Serve hot with cooked jasmine rice.

Serving Suggestion: Thai Pineapple Chicken Curry is traditionally served with jasmine rice. Enjoy with a side of Thai-style cucumber salad or steamed vegetables for a flavorful and satisfying meal.

Recipe 58: Jamaican Brown Stew Chicken

Preparation Time: 15 minutes

Cooking Time: 45 minutes
Total Time: 1 hour
Servings: 4

Ingredients:
- 1 lb chicken pieces (legs, thighs, or breast)
- Salt and pepper to taste
- 2 tablespoons vegetable oil
- 1 onion, chopped
- 2 cloves garlic, minced
- 1 bell pepper, chopped
- 1 carrot, sliced
- 1 tomato, chopped
- 2 tablespoons brown sugar
- 2 tablespoons soy sauce
- 2 tablespoons ketchup
- 1 tablespoon Worcestershire sauce
- 1 teaspoon dried thyme
- 1 teaspoon paprika
- 1/2 teaspoon ground allspice
- 1/2 teaspoon ground cinnamon
- 1/2 teaspoon ground nutmeg
- 1 cup chicken broth
- 2 tablespoons vinegar
- 2 green onions, chopped
- Cooked rice for serving

Instructions:
1. Season the chicken pieces with salt and pepper.
2. Heat vegetable oil in a large skillet over
medium-high heat.
3. Add the chicken pieces to the skillet and brown on
all sides. Remove from the skillet and set aside.

4. In the same skillet, add chopped onion, minced garlic, chopped bell pepper, and sliced carrot. Cook until softened.
5. Stir in chopped tomato, brown sugar, soy sauce, ketchup, Worcestershire sauce, dried thyme, paprika, ground allspice, ground cinnamon, and ground nutmeg.
6. Return the browned chicken pieces to the skillet.
7. Pour in chicken broth and vinegar. Bring to a simmer.
8. Cover and cook for about 30 minutes, or until the chicken is cooked through and the sauce thickens.
9. Adjust seasoning with salt and pepper if needed.
10. Garnish the Jamaican Brown Stew Chicken with chopped green onions.
11. Serve hot with cooked rice.

Serving Suggestion: Jamaican Brown Stew Chicken is traditionally served with rice and peas. Enjoy with a side of steamed vegetables or fried plantains for a taste of Jamaica.

Recipe 59: Lebanese Garlic Chicken (Djaj Mhammar)

Preparation Time: 20 minutes
Marinating Time: 1 hour
Cooking Time: 30 minutes
Total Time: 1 hour 50 minutes
Servings: 4

Ingredients:
- 1 whole chicken, cut into pieces
- Salt and pepper to taste

- 1/4 cup lemon juice
- 1/4 cup olive oil
- 10 cloves garlic, minced
- 1 teaspoon ground cumin
- 1 teaspoon paprika
- 1/2 teaspoon ground cinnamon
- 1/2 teaspoon ground allspice
- 1/4 teaspoon ground cloves
- 1/4 teaspoon ground nutmeg
- Chopped fresh parsley for garnish
- Lemon wedges for serving

Instructions:
1. Season the chicken pieces with salt and pepper.
2. In a large bowl, whisk together lemon juice, olive oil, minced garlic, ground cumin, paprika, ground cinnamon, ground allspice, ground cloves, and ground nutmeg to make the marinade.
3. Add the chicken pieces to the marinade and toss to coat evenly. Cover and refrigerate for at least 1 hour, or overnight for best flavor.
4. Preheat the oven to 375°F (190°C).
5. Arrange the marinated chicken pieces in a baking dish.
6. Bake in the preheated oven for about 30 minutes, or until the chicken is cooked through and golden brown.
7. Garnish the Lebanese Garlic Chicken with chopped fresh parsley.
8. Serve hot with lemon wedges on the side.

Serving Suggestion: Lebanese Garlic Chicken (Djaj Mhammar) is traditionally served with rice pilaf or Arabic bread. Enjoy with a side of fattoush salad or hummus for a delicious Lebanese meal.

Recipe 60: Turkish Chicken Iskender

Preparation Time: 20 minutes
Cooking Time: 40 minutes
Total Time: 1 hour
Servings: 4

Ingredients:
For the Chicken:
- 1 lb chicken breast or thigh, thinly sliced
- Salt and pepper to taste
- 2 tablespoons olive oil
- 2 cloves garlic, minced
- 1 teaspoon paprika
- 1 teaspoon ground cumin
- 1 teaspoon ground coriander
- 1/2 teaspoon dried oregano

For the Tomato Sauce:
- 2 tablespoons tomato paste
- 1 cup tomato puree

- 1 teaspoon paprika
- 1 teaspoon ground cumin
- Salt and pepper to taste
- 1 tablespoon butter

For Serving:
- Cooked rice or Turkish bread
- Yogurt for drizzling
- Butter for drizzling
- Chopped fresh parsley for garnish

Instructions:
1. Season the chicken slices with salt, pepper, minced garlic, paprika, ground cumin, ground coriander, and dried oregano. Toss to coat evenly.
2. Heat olive oil in a skillet over medium-high heat. Add the seasoned chicken slices and cook until golden brown and cooked through. Remove from the skillet and set aside.
3. In the same skillet, add tomato paste, tomato puree, paprika, ground cumin, salt, and pepper. Cook until the sauce thickens.
4. Stir in butter and remove from heat.
5. To assemble, place cooked rice or Turkish bread on serving plates. Top with the cooked chicken slices.
6. Pour the tomato sauce over the chicken and rice or bread.
7. Drizzle with yogurt and melted butter.
8. Garnish with chopped fresh parsley.
9. Serve hot.

Serving Suggestion: Turkish Chicken Iskender is traditionally served with rice or Turkish bread. Enjoy with a side of shepherd's salad and pickled vegetables for a delightful Turkish dining experience.